LINCOLN CHRISTIAN COLLEGE AND S

W9-BVG-099

KEEP IT REAL

KEEP IT REAL

Working with Today's Black Youth

EDITED BY

Anne E. Streaty Wimberly

Abingdon Press
Nashville

KEEP IT REAL
WORKING WITH TODAY'S BLACK YOUTH
Copyright © 2005 by Abingdon Press

All rights reserved.

No part of this work may be reproduced or transmitted in any form or by any means, electronic or mechanical, including photocopying and recording, or by any information storage or retrieval system, except as may be expressly permitted by the 1976 Copyright Act or in writing from the publisher. Requests for permission can be addressed to Abingdon Press, P.O. Box 801, 201 Eighth Avenue South, Nashville, TN 37202-0801, or emailed to permissions@abingdonpress.com.

This book is printed on acid-free paper.

Library of Congress Cataloging-in-Publication Data

Keep it real : working with today's Black youth / edited by Anne E. Streaty Wimberly.
   p. cm.
Includes bibliographical references.
ISBN 0-687-49702-7 (pbk. : alk. paper)
1. Church work with African American youth. I. Wimberly, Anne Streaty, 1936–
BV4468.2.A34K44 2005
259'.23'08996073—dc22

2005014384

All Scripture quotations, unless noted otherwise, are taken from the *New Revised Standard Version of the Bible*, copyright 1989, by the Division of Christian Education of the National Council of the Churches of Christ in the United States of America. Used by permission. All rights reserved.

05 06 07 08 09 10 11 12 13 14—10 9 8 7 6 5 4 3 2 1

MANUFACTURED IN THE UNITED STATES OF AMERICA

With gratitude for the vitality and hope
shown by the
2003 and 2004 classes
of
The Youth Hope-Builders Academy
of Interdenominational Theological Center
and for all black youth who strive for
a future with hope

272
88

112086

Contents

Preface

This book proposes a comprehensive framework for ministry with today's black youth. It is intended to invite open and honest consideration of what constitutes relevant, authentic, vital, and growth-producing work with black youth. The framework builds on the image of the congregation as a "village" wherein leaders and parental figures "keep it real" with youth and themselves by opening a space for conversation and guidance on tough issues and by calling themselves to accountability. The book takes seriously the voices of black youth and the unique and complex concerns faced by them and those who rear the youth in our fast-paced, techno-saturated, consumer- and hip-hop–oriented culture where racism still abounds. The goal of helping youth grow as Christian hope-builders is central to real ministry with them and pivotal to the mentoring and modeling functions of adults in the "village."

The chapters in the book represent the collaborative work of scholars who have held leadership roles in the Youth Hope-Builders Academy of Interdenominational Theological Center in Atlanta, Georgia, and in youth ministries elsewhere. Each scholar continues to serve in youth programs in various capacities and is passionate about what must happen to make ministries with black youth come alive for the sake of these youths' present and future leadership in the church and world.

We have written this volume expressly for the many adults who touch the lives of youth, including pastors, youth ministers, church members, parents, and other family members. Our invitation is also for adults and youth to engage in conversation together about the material included here and to discuss together the questions appearing at the end of each chapter. Our hope is that this volume will stimulate conversation, reflection, and action on the imperative need for real ministry with youth and the essential role of congregations in making it happen.

No volume unfolds without the help of caring and inspiring others. We wish to extend enormous gratitude to ninety-six high school participants in the Youth Hope-Builders Academy whose insights and unabashed challenge to adults to "be real" inspired much of the writing herein. Additional appreciation goes to numerous unnamed youth with whom the authors have ministered and shared stories of struggle and hope. Many hours were willingly and tirelessly given by Dr. Edward Wimberly, who read, reviewed, commented, and helped to edit chapters in the book. His own concern for youth and his desire for their journeys of promise have shown through his persistent help and stimulating conversations as my own editing process unfolded. I am immensely thankful for his abiding presence and support. Tremendous gratitude is also due the Lilly Endowment Incorporated, which provided generous funding for the Youth Hope-Builders Academy.

Anne E. Streaty Wimberly, Editor

The Challenge and Promise of Real Ministry with Black Youth

Anne E. Streaty Wimberly

The truth must be told, however harsh it may be; it may redden your eyes, but it won't blind you.

—Ahmadou Kourouma, Ivorian writer,
from *The Suns of Independence*, 1968[1]

Today's black youth are challenging the church to give concrete attention to the kind of ministry with them that is able to keep it real. The importance of this challenge was powerfully revealed during a youth and family forum in a church in Decatur, Georgia. During that event, a thirteen-year-old girl told a multigenerational panel about critical issues faced by black youth in her school and about hurtful responses to concerns they raised with school officials. She expressed her dismay at negative views and treatment of black youth in and beyond the school that she felt impinged on black youths' forming a sense of self-worth.

A grandmother responded to the youth with words of assurance, guidance, and affirmation. In her sharing, this community sage told part of her own story of maltreatment not simply in our society where racist ideologies prevail but also in the home of her childhood where, as a stepchild, she was not affirmed and was on the receiving end of abusive language. Her final words to the young teen were these: "You are a precious child of God. You are beautiful. I love you, and I want you to know God loves you too. Don't you let nobody turn you around." Other panelists followed with suggestions to the youth as well as to the parents and others gathered in that "village" about ways of confronting the kinds of blocks to black personhood shared by the teen.

In that youth and family forum, the youth experienced the welcome of shared story and received the kind of presence and empathic protective care and nurture that typify what may be called "village" functions. The forum became a communal space where extended family members dwelled together and formed an authentic habitus of connectedness and belonging. The attention of the community focused on "keeping it real." And, in its process of "keeping it real," this community inspired hope by providing a "picture" of the valued adolescent self and a vision of self-efficacy that teens and adults alike needed for the journey ahead.[2]

In a contrasting situation, I heard the story of a parent who called a radio talk-show host about her son. The parent was distraught about her teenaged son's insistence on his own choice of what she viewed as objectionable apparel, hairstyle, music, and language. She added that her appeal to him to at least wear a "Sunday suit" to church resulted in his strong response, "Who needs the church anyhow? I've got to be real!" Fearing that his chosen demeanor would make him a target for police profiling and thwart job opportunities, the parent pleaded for answers to resolve the daily heated family debates and parental fear of losing her son to an unsafe world and problematic future.

The cry of black youth for "realness" and the need of churches to respond to this cry are not new. Throughout the twentieth century there was a necessary plea for genuineness in adults' relationship with youth, authenticity in adults' behavior as Christians, and relevance in ministries with and on behalf of youth.[3] But there are multiple unique qualities of the current generation of black adolescents that require new responses that "keep it real." These young people are part of the first generation of youth born during the time of a media technology explosion marked by the Internet, cell phones, DVD players, CD writers, cable television in homes, satellite television in schools, and advanced interactive gaming systems.[4] However, black youths who do not come from an abundant socio-economic location have least accessibility to the wide range of technology and the beneficial technology know-how derived from this access.[5] Nonetheless, black youth are exposed to more TV media content than youth in other racial groups. It is also fair to say that all youth are immersed in media that overexposes them to a plethora of violence, sex, crime, and consumer enticements.[6]

Black youth are unique in their disproportionate representation among the poor and jobless, among school dropouts, in single-parent households, in foster care, and in youth detention facilities. They are more apt to engage in sexual activity at earlier ages than other youth.[7] At the same time, black student high-school completion rates have continued to increase over the past two decades; and [black youth] are "less likely to engage in alcohol and drug use—and more likely to engage in community service than youth of other racial groups."[8] Likewise, black youth show distinctive patterns in the area of religion. While the actual proportion of black youth who are unchurched is unknown, studies show that religious faith and activity are highest among black adolescents compared to those in other racial groups. Black youth are also more likely to pray daily than adolescents in other groups. Moreover, more black Protestant youth than youth in other racial groups identify themselves as born-again Christians.[9] An important finding across all groups of youth is that the majority are not alienated from or hostile toward organized religion, although girls are more likely than boys to assign importance to it. They go to church where friends are affiliated. They seek a relational experience there and want to share their experiences with someone they know and trust. The large number comprising the present generation of adolescents will provide the church with unparalleled opportunity for evangelism and discipleship. But, again, new approaches will be needed to reach the youth.[10]

The complex mix of race, language, class, gender, family configurations, values, beliefs, attitudes, and behaviors found in the overall group of current and upcoming groups of adolescents led to the name "the Mosaic generation" (those born between 1984 and 2002). Although there is similar complexity among black youth, the experience of racism is common and unique to all of these youth. Beverly Tatum reminds us that "for Black youth, asking 'Who am I?' includes thinking about 'Who am I ethnically and/or racially? What does it mean to be Black?' "[11] The question of identity that children entering adolescence raise is explored by black youth in racial terms.[12] This distinctive aspect of the lives of black youth requires ministry approaches that address it.

Meanings and Necessity of Keeping It Real in the "Village"

"Keeping it real" is a term used to indicate an engaged form of Christian youth ministry that intentionally brings to the forefront the concrete life experiences and concerns of youth.[13] It is a process undertaken by youth leaders, parents, and other adults to connect the realities of black youth life in and beyond our churches to the gospel message. The goal of "keeping it real" is to help youth see and embrace God's plan for their welfare and a future with hope (Jeremiah 29:11), and to make possible their development and spiritual growth resulting in their becoming Christian hope-builders in the church and world.

Accomplishing the goal requires recognition that black youth come from varied family circumstances, neighborhoods, schools, peer groups; and they have formed beliefs and views of church and religion based on their observations, involvement, and attitudes of church members and others toward them. Keeping it real in the "village" also requires the willingness of those who lead and care for black youth to be hope-builders. These leaders serve as models of this role, and risk being transparent and vulnerable in order to make their experiences and life narratives visible for youth to see and want to emulate. The intent of the leaders' self-disclosure is also to create a safe environment for youth to share their stories.

Self-disclosive engaged approaches can be risky in the sense that they can open wounds requiring intervention by skilled practitioners. Nonetheless, they are essential in black youth ministries because they take seriously the youths' voices and stories from their social locations rather than viewing the youth *acontextually*. The approaches "keep it real" by assuring a youth-context-story process linkage in environments where youth find genuineness, openness, and committed caring leaders.[14] An example is the forum described earlier. Indeed, because of the difficult realities of black youth life today and black teens' search for belonging and deepening faith, this kind of engaged approach is more essential today than ever before.

The Challenge Before Us

Our youth are growing up in a culture where there is a growing search of persons for meaning, purpose, and love.[15] Historically, black churches and civic institutions helped black people address this quest by providing spiritual and other resources needed amidst life's trials and tribulations and dehumanizing treatment heaped upon us in wider society. Our churches were the places where everyone could go to feel genuine welcome, hospitality, and love. However, Cornel West makes the claim that, today, market-driven forces and market moralities have tended to undermine the connectional roots of the black church.[16] He concludes that market-driven forces are destroying black families, neighborhoods, schools, churches, and mosques. As a result, black youth and adults alike experience a new and pervasive socially decaying and fragile existence.[17]

In addition to what has been said earlier, the media culture also exerts formidable influence on all of us in the present market-driven culture. Joyce West Stevens reminds us that "the television media consistently fabricates and markets role models by means of dramatic and comedic storytelling and spectator sports."[18] She underscores the media's role as a socializing agent of values of materialism. We grasp from the media the urgency of material consumption and the attainment of material possessions to affirm material well-being.[19] Importantly, Stevens states further: "Common opinion is that television impacts the developmental trajectory of youth, especially in the domain of role model formulation."[20]

Adults also develop perceptions and attitudes about teen culture through mass media, sensationalism, marketing, and entertainment that result in their devaluation of youth. In fact, Sharon Nichols and Thomas Good contend that adults' "attitudes toward youth have grown more critical over time" because of problematic media portrayal of teen culture.[21] These attitudes have been revealed by a sizable number of adults' use of negative adjectives, such as *rude, irresponsible,* and *wild* in two studies, and by worry expressed by "parents and non-parents alike about what they saw as youths' growing character deficits."[22]

There is need for caring and affirming "village environments" that counter adults' devaluation of youth and that incorporate engaged ministry approaches. This need is also clearly highlighted by our youths' consciousness of a "missing ingredient" that prevents them and others from having a feeling of "home." They, along with others across the generations, are in search of that missing ingredient. The intensity of this search is reflected in the yearly increase in attendance of youth, family members, and church and community leaders at the Annual Youth and Family Convocation of Interdenominational Theological Center (ITC) in Atlanta, Georgia. From its inception in the early 1990s, the number of participants has steadily climbed to well over two thousand. Similar increases are being noted in the quarterly forums that are part of the Youth Hope-Builders Academy, an ITC program for high school youth. Participants come from middle-class and poor families; urban, rural, and suburban settings; differing church sizes; and the full range of denominations. They come to foster their recognition that

- individuals and family units are not alone;
- there is strength in attacking together the common issues;
- common solutions derive from shared insights;
- cross-generational sharing and celebration of family and community enhance life together; and
- youth and family members can be empowered to act on principles, values, skills, and strategies.

The work of Andrew Billingsley, chronicled in *Climbing Jacob's Ladder: The Enduring Legacy of African American Families*[23] and in the book *Mighty Like a River*, [24] corroborates the quest of black people to reclaim historic values and a sense of community for the sake of our youth and future generations. Billingsley is clear in his assertion that our families, along with our churches, must be principled actors in this process. In his book *Restoring the Village, Values, and Commitment: Solutions for the Black Family*, Jawanza Kunjufu raises the critical question: "When a home breaks down, who in the village will rescue the children?"[25] He also calls to our attention the historic cultural understanding that "the black family is more than father-mother-sister-brother."[26]

Jack and Judith Balswick, in their book *The Family: A Christian Perspective on the Contemporary Home*, are clear in describing the impact of modernity on family issues and the disintegration of traditional communities. Although they are not African American, their assessment of the current ethos certainly applies to black families and the plight of youth within them. The Balswicks target a prevalent fragmentation of consciousness by stressing the negotiation individuals undertake "between the impersonal competition of the marketplace and the intimacy of friendship and family and between rationality in the school and faith in the pew."[27] We also enter into negotiations between the fast-paced solutions of television and a broad range of other techno-gadgets and the routine open-endedness of daily face-to-face life.[28] The Balswicks make clear that "the fragmentation of consciousness has produced a crisis in the areas of morality and authority within the family. Each family must construct its own value system, usually without the support of the extended family."[29]

The tendency of family members to go in separate directions with little time given to communication compounds the sense of disintegration of family and community life. Moreover, it is certainly the case that communication has also become exceedingly complex to the extent that much of what we call the generation gap, or the gap between adults and youth, is largely a gap in communication.[30] In view of all of these realities, it is not surprising that youth and family members alike are searching for a sense of community or "home" and opportunities to confront head-on the multiplicity of issues bombarding our youth and the adults who must guide them.

Importance and Promise of a Village Orientation

An important assumption underlying "real" work with black youth is that hope-building with black youth cannot be separated from the black family/extended family context. Families constitute the primary unit for the socialization of the young. Youth develop values, commitments, views of self, and styles of relating in their families. Families are cornerstones of the youths' identity development.

Families are also places where youth experience tremendous struggle, woundedness, and even violence. And they are environments where parents or guardians experience the same and reach out for healing and answers to questions about how to parent their teens. Consequently, youth ministry that seeks to "keep it real" cannot neglect the inclusion of the very family contexts out of which youth come and will return.

The "village," as it is being used here, is an African ancestral image of family patterns that is set forth in a revered Akan proverb: "It takes a village to raise a child." *Village* connotes patterns of communal solidarity, guidance, and support out of which can come a valued identity and hopeful life direction in the midst of racism and other trials and tribulations of black life. Attention has already been given to critical issues our youth and families face today that have contributed to the loss of "village" functions or the deconstruction of a communal sense of who we are. What we want to make clear in this book is that it will be extremely difficult to make a helpful and lasting impact on our youth, their movement toward a hopeful future, and their wearing the mantle of hope-builder. But we *must* make every effort to do so.

We must also recognize that the local congregation as village has a vital role to play in the restoration of village functions. We must take seriously what was said above about the fragmentation of consciousness, which has led to a crisis of authority and morality. Part of the fragmentation is the reality that there are many conversations that vie for the attention of youth, and these conversations define for them what is real. What is real from the faith perspective must also be part of the youth-context-story-process linkage if congregations are to make an authentic contribution to youths' formation of a spiritual foundation for their lives. The local congregation is essential in providing an alternative voice to those that bombard them on a daily basis.

The significance of the local congregation is that it can also help youth grasp and act on the New Testament biblical faith in which what is real involves God's intentions for their lives that is revealed in the life of Jesus Christ. What is real is what God through Jesus Christ and the Holy Spirit are making manifest to us on a daily basis. The real is not only the world as we see it but also the world as God intends it, which is to make manifest God's desire for the wholeness of persons and families and for a beloved community where love, peace, and justice abide. We as a people have an important role in modeling this plan of God. Likewise, as leaders in today's and tomorrow's world, our youth have a role to play; and one of the village functions of local congregations is to help youth to discern and prepare to take their place in God's plan for transforming the world to what is real in God's eyes. While the reality of the world may be driven by market forces and the fragmentation of consciousness, the "real" from God's perspective is a world living under the purposes of God. Youth must be helped to see that they have an important role to play in carrying out this purpose. Indeed, our youth become true hope-builders when they become impassioned by what they see and learn from adult models and mentors to embrace the realities of growing up in Christ and to live the Christian lifestyle in the world. This is, in fact, the promise of real ministry with black youth.

A Way Forward

Keeping it real will require specific actions on the part of black churches in order for youth to see church as vital to them and what goes on in our churches as an important foundation for their present and future lives. The contents of this book reveal several key interrelated actions that will be described briefly here.

The first action is our embrace of adolescence as a gift, God's gift. The prevailing bout among adults that is called "ephebiphobia,"[31] or a fear and loathing toward adolescents resulting in devaluation of them and views of adolescence as a problem, must be overcome. A way of overcoming it is by embracing what Eugene Peterson describes as "a strong Christian conviction, substantiated by centuries of devout thinking and faithful living, that everything given to us in our bodies and in our world is the raw material for holiness. Nature is brought to maturity by grace and only by grace. Nothing in nature—nothing in our muscles and emotions, nothing in our geography and our genes—is exempt from this activity of grace. And adolescence is not exempt."[32] Affirming our youth as God's gift also means that we see ourselves as wholly involved in their lives and that we welcome them in ours, knowing that this presence together does not preclude pain and bewilderment but that it, nonetheless, opens the way for them and us to grow up in Christ.[33] Indeed, as Peterson puts it, when we "accept adolescence as a gift from God, bright new areas of hope open up, fresh energies of love are released, vital surges of faith erupt."[34]

The second action is for us to make room for the youth-context-story process mentioned earlier. There is much to be discovered about our youth that they really want to share with us. We must take seriously our responsibility to hear their concerns and understand the issues that are important to them. Our youth are calling for attention. And it is not so much a "notice me" attention as it is the kind of attention that validates the importance of their lives, experiences, feelings, and intentions.[35] Indeed, helping black youth to grow up in Christ requires us to listen to their stories in affirming and safe environments where they can build positive identities, develop talents and strengths, and envision and prepare for their role as hope-builders in today's and tomorrow's church and world. In our presence *with* them and listening *to* them, we will be able to see the personal, cultural, and social assets they have that are often neglected or underutilized. A fundamental goal of the youth-context-story process is to assure youth that we care about them, their fullest awareness of who and Whose they are, and their development of their potential for hope-building.

The third action is our response of gratitude for youths' critique of us. Youth boldly and frequently declare that adults are guilty of hypocrisy. They point out in clearest terms that professed Christians fail to "walk the walk and talk the talk" while giving them moral guidelines to follow. This is painful for adults to endure, yet it is part of the adolescent's process of gaining ability to conceive moral principles. To use Peterson's words, "Adolescents are, as a class, moralists and idealists."[36] In adolescence, they move beyond uncritical acceptance of adult behaviors and directives. They move toward scrutinizing our behavior and questioning our authority using, by the way, the principles we have given them.[37]

We need not be afraid of the word *hypocrisy*, but rather look for the truthfulness of its application to our lives and address our own needs for growth in Christ. For this reason, our response must be one of gratitude for the moral glasses through which our youth see us. Peterson describes gratitude as a response that signals our recognition of "a kind of testing device that sounds the alarm when hypocrisy is detected."[38] We need that because the sin of hypocrisy is one of the most difficult to detect in ourselves.[39] However, Peterson goes on to say that "simply because adolescents sometimes speak in moral tones they suddenly acquire moral authority. Their insights do not suddenly catapult them into a position of superiority. Finding stupidity, intransigence, and evil where they did not expect it . . . [in us] is only the beginning of their moral education. Someday they will find it in themselves; and when they do they will no longer be kids."[40]

The fourth action entails our intentionally becoming mentors to our youth, and models of the Christian faith we expect them to emulate. Mentoring must be at the heart of youth ministries that "keep it real." Our youth need our presence with them, and the knowledge, insight, counsel, and nurture that come from wise adults. And they are looking for adults who are willing to commit to being involved in their lives on a consistent basis. Mentoring lies at the heart of "village" functions and at the center of an essential requirement in black churches and communities to confront the missing ingredient that is preventing our youth—in fact all of us—from feeling a sense of human connectedness and "home." In his insightful critique of the black community's disintegration of a sense of peoplehood, Asa Hilliard also suggests priorities for action to reverse this situation. Modeling is one of them.[41] In order to promote black youths' development of the Christian lifestyle and a hope-building way of being and acting in the world, we must model it. Hilliard's words are particularly salient: "We are not true role models for our children until we consciously order our lives to serve that function."[42] But he adds to modeling the key elements that bring together the mentoring and modeling functions of the village. These elements include showing unconditional respect for our youth by listening to and observing them closely; holding them responsible for real and important things; giving them mature feedback on what they do; providing appropriate recognition for their efforts; and expressing love to them as they struggle to become mature adults.[43]

Finally, taking action that provides a foundation for the present and future lives of black youth necessarily includes parental figures in ministries with them. Those who are rearing teens often struggle with what to do, how to do it, and whether to do what they think they should do. They want direction in carrying out their distinctive task of parenting black youth in today's world. And they need assurance that the ministry they undertake as parents holds promise for their continuing growth as persons, parents, and followers of Jesus Christ. Real youth ministry assumes that youth belong to and grow up in families and that the heads of those families must not be disqualified from the important role they play in contributing to the youths' present and in determining their future. Ultimately, keeping it real helps parental figures to know that their main job is "to be a person." There are no techniques to master that will make a person a good parent. There is no book to read that will give the right answers. The parent's main task is to be vulnerable in a living demonstration that adulthood is full, alive, and Christian.

The Invitation to Read Further

The book is organized in two parts. Part One is called "Welcome to Our World: Hearing, Seeing, and Responding from Inside Teen Life." The three chapters in this part invite us into the lives, issues, and thoughts of black youth, and the implications of them for youth ministries. Specifically, the chapters explore responses to the question: *How may we engage in ministries with and on behalf of black youth in ways that "keep it real?"* Chapter 1 is entitled "The Gift of the Youth: The Hope of the Church." Written by Herbert R. Marbury and Annette R. Marbury, the chapter addresses the promise of black youth and ministry with them through a biblical and current-day exploration of the gifts they bring to community. Youth are presented as persons of insight whose observations, critical thoughts, and challenge are gifts that can feed the community's passion to make a better world.

Chapter 2 focuses on "A Matter of Discovery." In it, Philip Dunston and I emphasize that real ministry with black youth requires attentiveness to how youth see themselves and to what youth have to say to adults about their own lives. The chapter reveals a picture of black teen life challenges, fears, and hopes; and it provides a theological framework for responding to the youth.

"Getting Real" is the title of chapter 3. In this chapter, Maisha I. Handy and Daniel O. Black invite us into a frank conversation about realities in the lives of black youth that must not go unnoticed. These authors also offer a forthright critique of churches' ofttimes indecisive and insufficient action in matters of critical life questions and taboo topics raised by youth and needing forthright response.

Part Two highlights the topic "Called to Lead, Staying the Course." The three chapters in this part of the book draw attention to a framework and concrete approaches to be undertaken by churches and parental figures as part of youth ministries that "keep it real." In chapter 4, "Called to Parent: Parenting as Ministry," Elizabeth J. Walker presents a biblical, theocultural, and pastoral framework for parenting, and essential parenting functions and tasks to be used in ministry and family settings.

Chapter 5 is entitled "Hope in the Midst of Struggle: Church and Parents Together in Raising Teens." Written by Tapiwa Mucherera, the chapter explores the kinds of tensions arising between parental figures and today's teens and provides guides for addressing the tensions not only within the church as "village" but also in a variety of family settings found in black communities today.

Written by Michael T. McQueen, chapter 6 makes clear that "The Teens Are Watching." He directs pointed attention to the imperative role of pastors and all other adults as intentional models of the Christian lifestyle. He calls for a paradigm that provides real direction to the kinds of behaviors and conditions that allow this lifestyle to come alive in consistent ways to the end that teens will see them, embrace the values undergirding them, and emulate them.

The book ends with an Epilogue, "Keep It Real: Claim Hope for Tomorrow," that presents the voices of youth who participated in the Youth Hope-Builders Academy of Interdenominational Theological Center. These youth remind us of the hope that lies in them and the hope they have in the adults who strive to "keep it real" in ministries with them and on their behalf.

PART ONE

Welcome to Our World: Hearing, Seeing, and Responding from Inside Teen Life

CHAPTER 1

The Gift of the Youth:
The Hope of the Church

Herbert R. Marbury and Annette R. Marbury

*People were bringing their children to him in order that he might touch them;
and the disciples spoke sternly to them. But when Jesus saw this, he was indig-
nant and said to them, "Let the little children come to me; do not stop them; for
it is to such as these that the kingdom of God belongs."*

—Mark 10:13-14

Introduction

This chapter is written in collaboration with my mother and is
intended as a model for intergenerational partnership. Annette R.
Marbury is a lifelong church member and has been active in ministry with young people for several decades, serving in various
capacities. She is curious to know who the youth are today whose
rights and freedoms she struggled for in her early adulthood. She
grew up in the segregated South and was an activist in the Civil
Rights Movement. She was an instrumental part of my growth
from childhood to adulthood, and remains a wise parent and sage.

Our writing styles are different and so are our theologies.
However, since we advocate the intergenerational connection in
our discussion, we believe it only fair that we attempt to model it
in some fashion ourselves. In what follows, we will focus attention
on gifts black youth bring to our faith communities. In particular,
we will center on the story of the five loaves and two fish in the

Gospel of John for what we can learn from it about the gifts of youth to the community. In addition, because of the emphasis here on intergenerational dialogue, we will present a synopsis of a conversation with four youth who spoke frankly about their concern for what is happening in today's church and world. Their disclosures reveal the depth of feelings of youth today and hope for the church and world, if their voices are heard and taken seriously.

Five Loaves and Two Fish: The Gift of a Youth[1]

The Gospel of John's story of the five loaves and two fish, full of potent symbolism, vivid imagery, and mystery, captivated the imaginations of the ancient Christian community.[2] Regarded highly by the Gospel writers, it is the only story to appear in each of the four Gospels. Both Matthew and Mark even report this story twice in differing variations.

At first blush, the feeding of the five thousand appears an unlikely story with which to frame a chapter about "keeping it real" in youth ministry. It is, after all, about Jesus' work with the disciples. But at the center of the narrative is a *paidarion*,[3] a young boy whom commentators often consider incidental to the story. Without this *paidarion*, however, Jesus would not have had the gift needed to feed the community.

The story opens at the Sea of Galilee. Jesus had been performing signs among the people. The crowd, amazed by his works, grew and followed him. It appears they had been following Jesus for a good while that day, for the narrator opens the dialogue with Jesus inquiring of Philip as to where he and the disciples might find bread for the people to eat. The question itself is telling. Jesus did not raise the prior question, that is, *should* they feed the crowd. No, the question's phrasing accepts that responsibility *a priori*. Rather, his question, according to the Gospel writer, simply probes Philip's willingness and capability to provide for the needs of the crowd (v. 5).

Posing the question to Philip signifies somehow that it is the disciples' responsibility as emissaries of Jesus to meet the needs of the people. Amazingly, Philip balks. He sees the enormity of the crowd, the paucity of his own resources, and he responds out of an acceptance of an economy of scarcity by retorting that even six month's wages would not be sufficient to feed the crowd. Philip

4

was helpless. He was aware of the problem, the hungry crowd, and that Jesus had charged him with meeting the need, but because he could not see beyond his own perspective he could only respond as he did. Another disciple, Andrew, initially responds positively by noting the presence of a young boy with five barley loaves and two fish. In his next phrase, however, Andrew dismisses the possibility of aid from the boy and resorts to Philip's helplessness saying, "What are they among so many people?" Ultimately, just as his counterpart Philip, Andrew is inept, unable to rise to Christ's call and to meet the needs of the people. At this juncture, the story turns and Jesus takes center stage. He takes what the young person has to offer, blesses it, and with it he feeds the people.

Jesus' activity in the story models a full appreciation of the youth's gift. First, in Jesus' request for the food and the boy's willingness to share his food there is an implicit dialogue between Jesus and the boy. One has to speculate that Jesus did not simply commandeer the bread and fish but that, when requested by Jesus, the boy offered them willingly. Note what the Gospel writer does not report about the boy. There is no report of the boy's refusal to share what he has. More important, the boy does not approach Jesus with the economic perspective that so limited the responses of both Philip and Andrew. It does not occur to him that he should also reply, "What are they among so many people?" That which an adult would consider logical or proper does not shape his response. It is unique to his perspective and social location.

Second, Jesus gives visibility to the boy's voice. By offering his food, the boy raises his voice in the prevailing discourse about the community's hunger. What he has is not much "among so many." Even so, Jesus does not dismiss his offer. To the contrary, Jesus assigns to it esteem and a value that places the boy's voice on par with Philip's and Andrew's. By accepting what the boy had to offer, Jesus claims his voice and his offer as worthy before the entire community.

Finally, in sharp contrast, the story juxtaposes Philip's and Andrew's inability and the child's willingness and ability, the failure of the disciples and the efficacy of the boy. Because of the boy's voice, his hunger, his willingness to share, and Jesus' activity of inclusion of the voice of a young person among those of his own disciples, the needs of the entire community were met. The boy not only gave a gift to the crowd but also gave the disciples an invaluable and unexpected gift as well. He modeled for them the possibility of engaging the needs of the people (in this case hunger) without the hindrances of concern for economy and propriety, but rather with the unabashed naïveté that naturally attends youth.

Through the act of feeding, the symbolism of the story comes alive. Bread, for John the Gospel writer, is symbolic of flesh. This story alludes to the Passover meal where Jesus calls the bread his body. For John, Jesus is the Bread of Life. Jesus calls his disciples to be fishers of people. For the ancient church, this call is related to the spiritual. Together, bread and fish represent body and spirit, the complete person. Jesus' feeding the crowd did not simply sate their physical hunger, but the meal satisfied perfectly—body and spirit.

Real Ministry and the Gifts of Youth Today

The story of Jesus' appreciation and acceptance of the youth's gift reveals a potent and relevant model for a very "real" role of youth in today's church and world. Just as the crowd hungered for Jesus' signs and followed after him in Galilee, crowds also hunger today for hope and healing. The needs of people today are evident to the church. Poverty ravages communities across the United States and the world. Racism plagues our society like an unshakeable scourge. War continues to rage in the Middle East and elsewhere with an ever-rising death toll. HIV/AIDS is the number one killer of black men ages twenty-five to forty-four and black women ages twenty-seven to forty-five. Sexism is rampant, while heterosexism and the questions of homosexuality threaten to rend the very fabric of the church. Christ's query to Philip and the disciples resonates with those who claim discipleship in this age. However, like Philip, the church finds itself often inept, incapable of meeting the needs of the people. Like the disciples, the contemporary church also raises questions of economy, logic, and propriety as defenses when faced with the dire needs of the community. Two thousand years ago a young boy heard the call and came forward with his lunch. In his willingness to raise his voice, he pressed to the fore the issue of the needs of the people and the church's inability or unwillingness to meet those needs.

What are the voices of our young people saying today? What gift do they bring to the church and to the task of ministry? How might we allow their voices—unburdened by our inhibitions, our political correctness, and our concern for our positions, our power, our statuses, our reputations, and our finances—to speak to us? How might we become beneficiaries of their gifts in the same way that the disciples and the crowd were on the day of the miracle?

If we are to answer the questions fully, then we must surely accept the reality that gifts come in an inclusive community and there is a current mandate for an inclusive ministry. Carl Sandburg, in words contained in one of his poems, provides a cogent perspective of inclusiveness that

> There is only one Maker in the world
> and his children cover the earth
> and they are named All God's Children.[4]

Jesus' model of inclusive ministry invites our self-critique and action. Jesus' ministry, as depicted in the Gospel, is limited only by human frailty, the incomplete community, and the choice not to accept what he offers. Even with the best intentions, fractured communities often fail to provide solutions to obvious and urgent problems of the moment. "Where will we get enough food to feed all of those people?" Philip was absolutely certain that his fiscal resources were insufficient for the need. While Andrew had appropriately done the research, he also reported that what he found was equally insufficient. Jesus, however, was well aware that the solution to the human need would require the entire community, the boy and the disciples, the youth and the adult, hearing one another and giving full acceptance to the gift that the young boy lifted in the midst of the community.

The first step to realizing the gifts young people bring to ministry is the creation of an inclusive community. Jesus' ministry as depicted in the Gospel models such inclusivity. Such a community within our churches is by nature intergenerational. The miracle happened that day in an intergenerational group with a corporate need. Inclusivity for today's society, with its satellite technology, streaming media, and real-time transmissions, only magnifies the significance of the last lines of Sandburg's poem, "There is only one Maker in all the world/and his children cover the earth/and they are named All God's Children." How might this inclusivity be enacted? There are three dimensions the Gospel story raises: the call is to (1) engage youth in the prevailing dialogue, (2) raise their voices to visibility, and (3) see their concerns as part of the concerns of the larger community and their gifts as blessings needed by the whole.

In her helpful congregational resource *Facing Forward in Older Adult Ministry,* S. Miriam Dunson argues for this type of intentional connection. She believes that the community of faith can model the values that grow out of our biblical and theological faith traditions. For Dunson, this includes leading the way in developing a growing respect for the dignity of all persons regardless of age, leading the way in helping persons to live their entire span of life abundantly and to the fullest extent of their capabilities, and shaping values and attitudes in society by addressing issues concerning the meaning of life.[5] Although Dunson intends that these values be modeled to invigorate older adult ministries, the same values easily apply to ministry with youth.

Edward A. Loder argues that ministries should not be compartmentalized. Churches cannot isolate one group from the whole, since people do not live in insolated sublets. Rather, humans live in systems, connected to one another. The American economy has had a terrible effect on the traditional extended family. Youth leave their families of origin and lifelong support networks to follow jobs, while their parents move from their communities of origin to retire. Such a generational shift calls for intergenerational understanding and solutions.[6]

Years ago families had no need to be intentional about relationships between generations. They could be taken for granted. Most people lived in the context of an extended family. Members of several generations lived in close proximity to one another, knew each other, and supported each other. The nuclear family, parents and children that once lived in multigenerational groups, now live in atomistic isolation. The new dynamic has had a dramatic effect on the intergenerational connection. Loder says: "Specifically, we live in a way that no longer allows for older people and young people to interact with one another. Our culture is poorer for it."[7]

With such a generational divide in today's society, the youth who hold the fish and bread have all been removed from within the church's domain. Since the church no longer hears them or sees them, but only creates compartmentalized ministry for them where they are not empowered to explore and use their gifts, the church no longer lives in ways that are theologically relevant to young people. Because their voices are oftentimes unheard or only heard outside of the church, such as in hip-hop music, for example, the church misses the gifts of an important part of the intergenerational connection.[8]

We simply cannot do relevant theology in isolation. The task of theology is not a private affair. It is always in some sense a community effort arising from the context of the community and meeting that community's needs.[9] For each human need, God depends upon the community to find the proverbial five loaves and two fish in a basket; and this "meal" can be given by a young person already in our midst and waiting to witness to Christ by meeting the challenges of our present-day world.

In theory, an inclusive, intergenerational community appears workable, but how might it look for the church? What questions might young people raise? Is the church ready for their gifts, as was the crowd in Galilee, or would the church rather go hungry? In order to answer the questions, it is important to hear the voices of youth.

Engaging the Dialogue: Giving Ear to Young Voices

Any discussion emphasizing the importance of an intergenerationally inclusive community would be sorely lacking without the real voices of young people. As chaplain at Clark Atlanta University, I hear daily the urgent questions and pressing concerns youth raise and seek to answer. In moments of sharing, I have become aware of the power of their message and know that it brings "food" for thought and action in the form of challenge and insight for our hungry world. Young people are worthy of our attention. As a result, the voices of several youth will be included here. Specifically, I gathered four students together for an informal conversation on the story of the five loaves and two fish. Focusing on that story, I raised the issue of the people's hunger and the disciples' inability to meet that need. In follow-up, agreement arose that our own communities have pressing needs that our churches either refuse to or are unable to address. We discussed how the young boy's gift not only fed the crowd but also forced the disciples to work with Christ to address the need of the community.

Ultimately, I asked the students to put into words some of the questions or concerns they would raise for the church's response. The issues they raised and those not raised surprised both Annette R. Marbury and me. Surprisingly, none of the four black youth raised the issues of racism or sexism, two topics that we both believed would rank somewhere in the conversation. Instead, three other issues quickly emerged from the discussion. The youth named "the church's schizophrenia on poverty," "the church's division on homosexuality," and "the church's silence on the war in Iraq." The refreshing unabashed naïveté with which they posed the issues was similar to the youthful qualities of the boy in the miracle story in the Gospel of John. And like the community in that story, the church today needs the youth who shared from their hearts about very real circumstances.

Engaging the dialogue is risky business. It calls us to make room at the table for unfamiliar, sometimes critical, and sometimes angry voices for which the community might not be ready. However, only when we can hear the voices with the critique of the young will we be in a position to receive the gift and provide needed nourishment to the community.

The Situation of the Poor: A Gift of Insight and Challenge

Not the first concern to be raised but one of the more poignant was their perception of the church's hypocrisy when it comes to the poor.[10] It was a concern formed by the firsthand experiences of one of the youth. Emblematic of the conversation, this student's statement presents the issue directly: "The church is hypocritical when it comes to its stance on poverty. It claims prosperity on one hand, and shuns and shames the poor on the other. Jesus never did this. Sometimes I feel like the members don't even look at me and my mother—like we're not even there." Incisive questions followed such as:

- "Why do we dress up for church? I know more people who would attend if they felt comfortable wearing what they have. Sometimes even I feel out of place."

- "Why do many prayers include the words 'poor and unconcerned' as if the two were synonymous?"
- "Growing up, we never had a nice car to drive to church. We always had to change churches because Dad and Mom could not afford to give for extra church causes and programs like those Men's and Women's Days. After we could not take any more embarrassment, we would leave."
- "When I was younger, I would wish that there was a church for poor people *only*, like me and my family. We would sing different songs, dress differently, and not have to pay a lot of money if we did not have it. Anybody could attend free."

As Annette R. Marbury, mother and seasoned youth worker, and I, campus minister, recounted the students' contributions to the discussion in preparing for this chapter, we thought, *What harsh words aimed toward the church—an institution to which we had given most of our lives!* But the dialogue with the youth raised an important and very real issue, that of the invisibility of the poor in our midst. A United Methodist bishop told a story some years ago that pointedly illustrates the student's concern; and although the bishop's story includes able responses by caring others, it still reminds us of what the student knows—in so many places, poverty still *is* and continues as though hidden and without response.

The bishop's episcopal area included Birmingham, Alabama. Realizing the significance of the city in the history of the Civil Rights Movement, the bishop led an ecumenical group effort to meet the needs of the poor throughout the city. The group agreed that their efforts would honor the ideals of Dr. Martin Luther King, Jr.

In the first year, the group agreed to donate to a center clothing to be distributed at Easter. As they distributed clothing, they noted that the people lacked shoes. The next year they donated new or used shoes. Even though the evaluation committee appointed by the bishop found that both years' efforts had been successful, the bishop believed that there was something lacking. So in the third year the committee organized an effort again for the donation of tennis shoes. Only this time the requirement was to come in person with new tennis shoes, as many pairs in various sizes as each person wished to donate. However, in order to give the shoes away, the donor had to be willing to wash the recipient's feet, place clean socks on them, look into their faces, see their grief, and listen to their stories of poverty. Those who participated in the bowl-and-towel experience claimed that something inwardly was transformed in the foot washing. Here, through close personal contact and intentional and meaningful dialogue, something was occurring. In his popular song "Basin and Towel," Michael Card calls to community to vow to enact this kind of soul-freeing and enlivening activity in any ordinary place and on any ordinary day. For Card, taking the vow is an act of humility that comes alive when one kneels and another yields. Jesus demonstrates how to do this

> through the will of the water
> and the tenderness of the towel.[11]

Both the bishop's story and the song poetically describe the importance of human connection and the community's solidarity with the poor. The faith community of Birmingham discovered through a small effort that those within the church could have meaningful relationships with those who were not within the church. In that exchange, they discovered the fish and loaves, gifts of compassion and connection. But the youth with whom I had conversation were crying out for care not yet given to those in need by Christians who deem themselves to be religious. At a deeper level, their cry was for the faith community to show the kind of maturity that comes from persons' experience with God and from their awareness of God's revealing Godself in all we do.

In our reflection on the student's cry, we recalled Howard Thurman's insight in *The Creative Encounter*: "For the Christian there are two principles in or parties to the religious experience. One is the individual himself, and the other is God. . . . In a religious experience, God meets the individual at the level not only of the individual's needs but also in my judgment more incisively, at the level of his residue of God-meaning and goes forward from there."[12]

The real-ness of the youth who told with great feeling the plight and invisibility of the poor in the Christian community evoked in us further thought. For us, the question surfaced: Who are the poor? In answering the question, we found ourselves confessing that we as adults are the poor because we have missed the message of what is intrinsic to our Christian belief. In far too many instances, our faith communities have not responded as fully as we should to the dire needs of the poor, and we have not heeded the voices of youth who see the state of our world that calls for response. To this extent we have missed God's call for the faith community to care, and have overlooked the example of Christ who received the gifts of barley loaves and fish from a youth. In this way we have developed limited vision, like that of Philip in the Bible story. The message is for us to become open to an encounter with God and God's call that comes through the presence and voice of youth.

As the dialogue continued, still further insights emerged. Out of the conversation came the view that, as the church, we have become so accustomed to traditions and rituals that teach us to preside *over* the cause of poverty, rather than to interact *with* the poor. The church creates committees, writes checks, and creates annual giving occasions in which youth have little to say and to which they have little to give. So, the question is raised anew: Who are the poor? In this case, an additional understanding of what it means to be "poor" emerged that highlighted the poverty of our youth. In our refusal to see them, hear them, and receive the gifts they want to give, we relegate them to a situation of poverty or deficiency in what they can do and give. The effect becomes worsened as they are criticized for what they do not do and are therefore charged as culpable for their own poverty.

In the conversation, the youth raised time and again the issue of compassion for the poor—the compassion that involves seeing real faces and making authentic connections. This includes compassion for them! Henri J. M. Nouwen illustrates this point in a helpful way: "Compassion removes all pretensions, just as it removes false modesty. It invites you to understand everything and everyone and to see yourself and others in the light of God and to joyfully tell everyone you meet, that there is no reason to fear."[13] Nouwen's perspective is that demonstrating this kind of compassion and understanding is not easy. Risks are involved. Real compassion involves our building a bridge to others "without knowing whether they want to be reached."[14]

In dialogue with the students, a powerful truth rang clear. The poor are more than simply people to whom we minister. The faces of the poor are also the faces of the youth not simply because they are adjudged deficient in what they have to give but because many black youth are economically destitute. They are young people who feel they have to camouflage their pain because their family's wages are insufficient to provide for basic needs like healthcare. They are ostracized by peers because there is no insurance to buy braces for dental correction. Sometimes their family's wages will not provide basic necessities like toothpaste, deodorant, or items for personal hygiene. Some students noted that being young and poor restricts their ability to attend important events such as an academic achievement ceremony because it is impossible to dress well enough. For others, poverty is accompanied by the hope that no one will invite them to the prom because they could never afford the fees, clothing, or other necessary accoutrements. Still others join gangs for the lure of economic gain, although illegal, and a sense of identity and self-esteem amidst what they experience as failure and hopelessness in the larger society.

Again, the question: Who are the poor? They are the youth who live daily with poverty. They are also the youth who have clear ideas about how the church neither welcomes nor hears them. They call us to think anew our work and to include their voices. As Christians, we are called to create a new paradigm. Young people must see their gifts as unique building blocks for God's reign, and experience God's joy in their collective voice within the local congregation. Only perhaps in the inclusive dialogue will we receive the youths' gifts of insight and challenge that are meant to bring about the release of fresh energies on behalf of the poor. Only then will the church find the barley bread and fish that so many of our youth want to share.

The Situation of Homosexuality: The Gift of Insight and Challenge

The conversation turned from poverty to a far more sensitive issue for the church, that of homosexuality. I quickly realized that these young people had far more exposure to the issues of sex and sexuality than I did at their age. They were more sophisticated in their understanding and more easily able to speak openly about the topic. Their questions, however, were basic and a fundamental challenge to the church's claim to moral authority.

The gift of these youth appeared in their push for a more inclusive community—a community committed to love, acceptance, and compassion, their invitation to form a welcome table around which to explore in-depth questions and thoughts such as "Why does my church treat homosexuals as outcasts? We claim that we are an open community, but we never really deal with the issue." "I'm not saying that homosexuality is right, but Jesus at least extended love to people." "I think it is right for people to be able to be themselves, however God created them to be. As a heterosexual, I can be myself. Why can't a gay person?" "Even if you don't think it's right, I have several gay friends, and they don't feel comfortable coming to church. They can't talk to their pastor because he's preaching about gays from the pulpit. They can't talk to their parents because their parents are so caught up in 'what the preacher says'."

Two months before I sat down to write this article, a student came to the chaplain's office to share with me that his older brother had "come out." He struggled with his brother's identity, the family's wholesale rejection, and their embarrassment in the church. As he told his story he was incredulous about his brother's sexuality, recalling stories of the older brother teaching him "how to date girls." His church's "love the sinner, hate the sin" response had been most problematic. Finally, he asked what should he do, believing that he had lost his best friend. My response to him was simply, "Love him—all of him. He is your brother." I explained to the student that he still had his best friend, only now his older brother probably needed him to show the love, compassion, and support that his family and church were unwilling to give.

The students, while comfortable with their convictions on the subject, did not share the same position. The conversation revealed the conflicted complexity of their positions and reflected the same conflict that rages in the church. Writer and former Clinton aide Keith Boykin chronicles the complex relationship between homosexuality and the black church. He notes particularly the disparity between the disparaging rhetoric of the pulpit and the acceptance many homosexual members often receive from the congregation.[15]

In our increasingly open and diverse society, it is difficult and even morally dishonest to ignore the issue of homosexuality, particularly when we do ministry with young people. As they navigate a world where they are free to raise questions about their own sexuality and raise questions about the sexuality of their peers, they continue to press the church for open and frank dialogue. They push the church where it is most vulnerable—in the places where we are uncomfortable with the dialogue, and our concerns for propriety, status, and reputation trump any genuine intention to engage in that risky conversation. In the absence of that type of inclusive conversation, our young people form troubling ideas about the motivations of the church.

One student commented that the church's vacillation on the issue of homosexuality was connected to financial concerns rather than moral ones. "Whenever the issue of homosexuality comes up, everybody dances around it because they don't want to offend those who contribute to the church's bottom line." What an indictment! If young people perceive the church to be motivated by profits over principles, then the church must address the issue of its own credibility in the lives of young people.

The comment may not be so far off the mark. In an interview, Boykin quotes a tongue-in-cheek comment made by the Reverend Rainey Cheeks, founder of the DC Unity Fellowship in Washington, D.C.: "Tell the whole church, for the next three months put your money in an envelope. If you're gay, lesbian, or bisexual, don't put any money in the envelope. See how much money you collect."[16]

Finally, one student raised the question based on an understanding of a biblical love mandate: "Isn't God supposed to be love; and if you can't love others, how can you love God? I just think people are people, and you should love them as they are."

In these questions, the young people do not ask the church to arrive at a final conclusion on the issue of sexuality; rather, they challenge the church to see the individual faces of those members of their own communities who should be able to look to the church for hope, acceptance, and love. What good gift can come of that? Are these the barley loaves and fish that the little boy offered that day?

Young people raise questions for the church about its silence, its lack of compassion, and its strict adherence to its own dogma. For them the question of love is simple. It is not mitigated by Philip's economy of scarcity. It does not acquiesce to fears about the loss of position or status. In the church's silence about the dissonance and the hatred masquerading as righteous piety, we lose credibility with our youth. They see the dissonance that we have trained ourselves to ignore.

Often, young people's perspectives on sexuality are deemed to be immature and naïve; yet at their young age they have a vocabulary to talk about issues of sexuality that many adults lack. By virtue of their social location, young people can bring insight for how the church can wrestle with and respond to issues of sexuality that their older counterparts do not have.

In the biblical story, Philip and Andrew fail to see what can be done to address the problem of hunger. Their social location leads them to a crippling pessimism. The young boy's offering, however, feeds the people and gives the gift of hope. Young people bring fresh insights and perspectives that, if received, can bless our people as well. Like the crowd that day, the contemporary church is being offered a gift. The crowd that day was hungry enough to receive fish and barley loaves. Young people raise questions to the church that is hungering today for the fullness of God's reign to be realized.

The Situation of War: The Gift of Insight and Challenge

Finally, the issue of war emerged in the conversation.[17] This topic was the shortest part of our dialogue. Nonetheless, the issue was present for them because they had college friends who had enlisted in the ROTC as their only means to attend school and who had been called to duty. Just as the opinions on the previous topics varied, so also did the opinions on war, ranging from the church's stance against war that is considered unjust to the poignant question and recall of a biblical mandate: "What about 'Thou shall not kill'?" "That's one of the Ten Commandments. I would rather oppose the government's decision to go to war than to oppose God."

In their sharing, the youth brought to mind what Sandburg's poem so aptly conveys about the world's becoming a smaller place. For them, youth who live where war is being fought are not some foreign people "over there." Instead, they are real human beings whose dying we see on the evening news. The conversation also highlighted that, in our shrinking world, we live next door to, dine with, go to school with, and play video games with immigrant youth from places being ravaged by war begun or entered into by our country. Moreover, American men and women who die in the heat of battle are not simply pictures on a televised report. They were fathers, mothers, sisters, and brothers from our neighborhoods.

What the youth had to say was telling and real. And again, in their telling they offered the gift of hard questions and thoughts often left buried in silence. Yet these are the very questions and thoughts that, if explored, have the potential to satisfy the hungering soul of the church and make possible the growth of all of us in the church.

Receiving the Gift of Youth: Building Hope for the Church

What is the gift of the youth? The young boy in the Gospel of John's story pushed the disciples, emissaries of the Christ, to see the hunger that they could not address. Philip was at the end of his resourcefulness. He had no money, no food. How could he respond to Jesus and feed the crowd? So he was silent. Andrew gave an excuse for his inability to meet the call of the Christ. While the responses were probably designed to protect the respective statuses and privilege of both Philip and Andrew in the eyes of Jesus and their peers, neither response was adequate. The people still hungered.

Youth today can be likened to the *paidarion* in the story, who had the gift needed to feed the community. In their thoughts and questions, youth today offer adults "food" for thought and exploration that, when heard and accepted, open a new sphere for the whole faith community's hope and vitality for vital faith to build. Their innocent, sometimes insolent, questions and thoughts test the relationship between youth and adults, and challenge the church to grow by holding the church accountable for real responses to Christ and ultimately to the people.

Jesus did something more miraculous that day than feed five thousand people. By allowing the boy to raise his voice in the discourse and by receiving the boy's fish and his barley loaves, Jesus set the model for meeting the needs of the community. Today, this model can be implemented only to the extent that the church allows all the voices of the intergenerational community to come to the table. By raising the boy's voice and contribution not simply to a place of visibility but to a place of importance and esteem, Jesus calls us to be intentional about hearing the voices of our young people and accepting openly the challenges they offer.

On the day of the miracle, the boy gave the disciples a gift. He pushed them to think beyond limits of the current discourse, to think beyond the scarcity of their resources, and beyond their own inadequacies. Somehow, for the boy, the hunger of the people mattered more than propriety. In his one audacious act of taking what little he had and offering it to the Christ, he challenged the disciples to do the same because the people were still hungry. Our own youth offer the same gift to the ministry of the church. The issues have changed, but the ofttimes stalled, stumbling, and stuttering response of the church recalls that of Philip and Andrew. If the church will hear the voices of young people, then we receive the hope that God has placed in our midst.

The charge then is for the church to accept the gifts of insight, questions, and critique that our young people bring. These gifts can become catalysts for addressing issues, concerns, brokenness—and yes, the hunger of the whole community for wholeness. Their gifts may seem little "among so many," but "little [does] become much when we place it in [Christ's] hands."[18] When we come to Christ with that which the entire community has to offer, then the miracle happens.

After our concluding moments of collaboration, my mother and I united with family around the dinner table. My three-year-old nephew and her grandson, Lawrence, the youngest member of our family and whom I see as part of the future generation of adolescents, joined the circle for prayer. My mother asked me to offer the blessing, and just as I was about to do so, Lawrence interrupted, "I want to say it, Uncle Herb." Before I could respond, he began in song with "God is great, and God is good . . . ." We accepted Lawrence's gift; it blessed our table and our family. More importantly, it reminded us that at three years of age he had already developed a voice. He spontaneously raised it in our presence, and Christ called us to receive it. May the church hear and welcome Christ's summons to receive the gift of our present–day youth and those to come.

Questions for Reflection and Discussion

1. What meanings do you assign to real ministry with youth? On what do you base these meanings?

2. What gifts of the youth are welcomed in your congregation? In what ways are the youths' questions and concerns voiced? What concerns are shared? What concerns do you think are kept unsaid? Why?

3. What attitudes and feelings do you have about the insights and challenges raised by youth in this chapter?

4. What needs to be done in your congregation to assure or enhance its seeing and welcoming the gifts of the youth within and beyond it?

CHAPTER 2

A Matter of Discovery

Philip Dunston and Anne E. Streaty Wimberly

A person is a person because of other persons.

—A South Soto proverb

Introduction

One day I was sitting in my office and three teenage members of my congregation walked in, handed me the abstract to a play, and said, "Dr. Dunston, here's something we would like to present." The title of the script was "So You Think You Know What It Is Like to Be a Teen? You Don't Have a Clue." Throughout the abstract, the teens made the point that it is difficult to articulate adequately all they are experiencing and the depth of their feelings about their lives. They confessed to being bombarded with numerous images and stereotypes of who they are, what they should be, and how they should act. As a result, there are times when teens don't know what or whom to trust. The play was their way of saying they want to share—they need to share—some of the realities of their lives from their perspective, not knowing if others were ready for it or, in fact, if they could trust others with what would be discovered. A central theme was their search for guidance, for validation as individuals, and the desire for some-one to step up and take notice.

My reading the abstract and viewing the play evoked much in me. I found myself asking, *Do we as pastors and congregations really have an idea what black teens are experiencing? Do we even care about their stories? Are we willing to hear black teens, engage them, and sup-port them in dealing with life's challenges? Are we really equipped to help them deal with their fears, guide them in overcoming obstacles con-fronting them, and assist them as they strive to become all they have been created to be?* The questions continue to burn within me. And it seems to me that answers to them are a pivotal matter of discovery.

This chapter explores and challenges pastors and congregations—all of us—to take seriously the real world in which today's black youth live and to heed their fervent cry to us to see them, hear them, and engage them lest we lose them. The chapter contains three emphases. First, we will present several stories of black teens for what we can discover about some of their current-day life challenges, fears, and hopes. Second, we will explore a theological framework for responses with and on behalf of our youth. We will give particular attention to a theology of presence, attentiveness, and compassion built from the themes in the stories. Finally, we will propose a para-digm of advocacy and strategic action on behalf of a hopeful present and future for our youth. The paradigm centers on the historical African cultural concept of the "village" and includes suggestions for hope-directed co-action of "village members"—black youth, their families, and the extended family of congregations and communities.

Our approach builds on the fervent call identified in the intro-duction for "real" hope-bearing ministry with youth. Our intent is to point a way toward keeping it real in black youth ministry. We will draw from insights gleaned from the Annual Youth and Family Convocation and the Youth Hope-Builders Academy for which Anne Wimberly served as leader, and Philip Dunston along with Maisha Handy as co-program coordinators, and to which the prologue has already referred.

Discovery Through Stories

Black youth want to tell their stories, and they both need and search for caring, trusted adults who will hear them. In fact, in order for black youth to tell their stories, there must be willing listeners who really *see them*, are *present with them*, and are ready to *respond to them*. These prerequisites for opening a place for story became vividly apparent in the ongoing initiatives called the Annual Youth and Family Convocation and the Youth Hope-Builders Academy. Beginning in the early 1990s, thousands of youth from a variety of backgrounds, cultures, socioeconomic statuses and denominational affiliations have participated in the convocations along with family members, and congregational and community leaders. From our stance on the leadership team, we have seen the importance of story-telling and story-listening, and the imperative need for the village to respond to critical issues in the lives of adolescents and their families such as violence; dying, death, and bereavement; grandchildren being raised by grandparents; influences of the media on youth and family life; sexuality and the Christian lifestyle; hip-hop culture; meanings of "walking the walk and talking the talk"; and the nature of the youth-friendly church.

The Youth Hope-Builders Academy includes an annual four-week summer residential program and year-round forums for youth, their families, and congregational and community leaders. The convocation, the residential program, and the forums provide numerous opportunities for black high-school youth to express openly and without judgment their stories and thoughts about the world, society, themselves, and others, including immediate and extended family. The engagement of the youth with caring listeners/mentors in heart-to-heart conversations and other opportunities to tell the self's story have further highlighted the importance and power of places for story. Moreover, this engagement has drawn attention to the needs of our youth to explore meanings of these stories for their lives as Christian sojourners.

Over the years of the convocation and the academy, numerous stories have surfaced. Though coming from different contexts, many of the stories contain related material and reveal similar themes. In what follows, aspects and themes of the lives of black teens will be presented in several case illustrations. The names of the youth depicted in these stories are fictitious. The stories highlight what congregations, families, and community leaders may not necessarily see, hear, or take seriously.

Michelle's Story: "We Want to Be Leaders, But Does It Matter?"

Michelle was very fond of the church where she grew up and where her parents were also members. Her father was a central figure in the church's music ministry. During her early childhood, Michelle began singing in the children's choir and had continued in the role of choir member across the years. While in school, she became interested in the guitar and, through lessons on an instrument purchased by her family, became a very proficient guitarist. She played in her high school's jazz band and performed with a small group at youth and other events. She tried to tell the youth leader that she really wanted a chance to play at church. She was told politely that it wouldn't look right for a female to play the guitar in church. Her father finally let her accompany a number for the youth choir, but she was coldly received by the congregation.

Michelle was not daunted by the adults' rebuff of the talent she wished to share. In fact, she with the support of other youth offered another approach. They asked the youth leader to seek an answer to their request: Why not let us form a praise and worship team that would be accompanied by the pianist, a drummer, and Michelle's guitar? Can't we be part of the devotional service on Sunday morning? They received a resounding "No!" After all, they were told, the devotional services prior to Sunday morning worship are always led by adult leaders in the congregation. The youth pressed further by asking if they could simply have the praise team present during an upcoming Sunday when the youth were to be in charge of the morning worship service. This request was granted, and the church really enjoyed both the service and the praise team. Michelle was overwhelmed. She had finally been given a chance to utilize her gift of leadership and musical talent in God's house. It was a major relief. But she and the other youth wondered why their gifts and talents had to be shared only during those times designated for youth only.

Michelle and several other youth asked the youth leader to approach the pastor again about incorporating them as praise and worship leaders at least one Sunday per month. She was not ready for what ensued. The church committee met to discuss the idea of a youth praise team. Michelle and the president of the youth group were invited to the meeting but were not allowed to say anything. The youth felt invisible and were visibly shaken by the sentiments of the church leaders that they were too young to lead worship. Finally, after the youth had taken all they could stand, they got up and ran out of the room. For a long time Michelle refused to return to that church, but later relented because of the friends she had there.

Tears came to her eyes as she told the story. For her, it was as though she were reliving the experience. She said, "People are always saying there's something wrong with youth today, that we're suppose to be leaders, but they don't see any leadership or, for that matter, anything good in us. Well, I wanted to lead in my church. So did the other youth. Was it wrong for us to want to lead at times other than just on youth Sunday? I don't understand it at all. It makes me angry."

Rick's Story: "Home? What Home?"

Rick told of looking for every chance he could to "escape" going home. He described home as an unhappy place—a place of discord where he, his mom, and siblings rarely get along. He described being addressed as a "silly, stupid boy" and as being just like his dad, whom he had never seen. The words "You're never going to amount to anything" are etched in his mind. Rick also conveyed his sense of dismay and hurt that the family goes to church every Sunday. In fact, attending church is a family requirement. With head bowed, Rick simply said, "Isn't church supposed to make a difference? In my family, it doesn't."

The youth group provides some of the "time-out" Rick craves. Although he feels that he cannot communicate with his mom, he finds the youth group a place to talk and a place of validation. He admires the youth leader and the leader's recognition of his speaking ability. Rick said that someday he might like to have a job where he could use his speaking ability. But he admits that the youth group is simply not enough. "After all," he said, "At the end, I still have to go home." His wish is to be able to talk with his mom, but doing so seems out of his reach. He said, "Sometimes I just want to die."

Yvonne's Story: "Being Black: There's a Problem"

Yvonne completed the required application and essay for the coveted international exchange program that was offered through her high school and from which three students would be chosen. Being chosen for the program would make possible her first international trip and opportunity to "get to know people in another part of the world up close," she said. Yvonne was now a junior and had remained an honor student throughout her school years. She had also been involved in a variety of community service activities throughout her high school years, including the times in which she tutored elementary schoolchildren and volunteered in a hospital nursery where she rocked babies born with drug addiction as the result of their mothers' addiction to crack cocaine.

Yvonne spoke of being very hopeful about her chances of being one of the youth chosen for the exchange program because she had been told that community service added significant points to the rating scale along with academic standing. Her hopes were dashed, however, when she was told that, although her academic standing was laudable, she had not done the kind of community service that "counted." She was not chosen. All of those chosen were white students, as had been the case in previous years. Moreover, she discovered that one of the three students had engaged in community service not too dissimilar from that of her own. And, the international vacation travels of the other two with their parents had been regarded as acceptable community service.

Yvonne spoke of being very disappointed at the outcome. This turn of events brought to mind other instances in which blocks to opportunities had occurred at that same school. She said, "I'm a good student. I do my best. It seems like that's just not good enough. I'll tell you one thing, though, I'm not going to give up."

Randy's Story: "Gang-banging Is Real"

Randy, now sixteen years old, was a gang member until he moved in with his grandmother across the country. Having no relationship with his biological father, and seeing his mother struggle to provide for the family, he sought to find love and acceptance outside of the home and community. Randy found that acceptance in the local neighborhood gang. At the tender age of fourteen, he had already been involved in drive-by shootings, rape, and acts of violence perpetrated against innocent people. The facial bruises and wounds on his body were a constant testament to the life he had come to know as gang warfare. The gang was where he found what he thought to be love and acceptance.

Randy confessed that most of the time he hated participating in gang activity. He really did not want to be part of the violent acts being committed by the gang. However, if he failed to defend the honor of the gang, he would bear the brunt of retaliation and be hazed himself. Randy also told of gangs of young girls that rivaled the gangs of young boys. The girls were noted for concealing razor blades underneath their tongues in order to render the blades undetectable. The young girls had mastered the art of "the flip," that is, at any given confrontational moment a girl could flip the razor blade from her mouth with such force that it would become an instant weapon to be used against the opposition.

Randy added that gang members were not your average cooperative students in school, either. In the community school he attended, there were constant instances of disrespect perpetrated against teachers and other students. "Of course," said Randy, "some [gang members] were expelled from school. I also had my share of detentions. And some went to jail. I guess I'm lucky. It could have been me."

Life Challenges, Fears, and Hopes of Black Youth

Three major themes appear in the stories of the youth. One theme focuses on youths' need for validation. The second draws attention to suffering engendered by oppressive circumstances. At the heart of the third theme is resilience. Each of these themes will be explored briefly.

YOUTHS' NEED FOR IDENTITY VALIDATION

A common theme in all of the stories is the need of youth for validation of themselves as persons of worth. Michelle sought validation from her church for her gift of leadership and musical talent. Rick wanted from his mother affirmation of his value as a person. Yvonne wanted to be recognized for her accomplishments as a black girl on par with white students in her school. Randy looked for validation from the peers in a gang.

Adolescence is a critical stage of life development when validation is immensely important. The work of psychologist Erik Erikson identifies adolescence as a period of crisis when young people go through a time of working out who they are, what they are going to be, and what they hope to make of their lives.[1] Carole Wade also states: "If youth navigate successfully through this period, they will emerge with a strong sense of identity."[2] However, "if they encounter major challenges, particularly from those in which they seek validation, they could sink into utter despair and become unable to make quality decisions about their own lives."[3]

The search for validation is also part of adolescents' meaning-making. Youth form meanings or make sense of themselves and their surroundings on the basis of the kind of recognition they receive from others in those surroundings. Importantly, they are not entirely passive in those circumstances. As we have seen particularly in the stories of Rick and Randy, youth consciously select alternate locations that hold promise for validation and positive meaning as substitutes for preferential ones—typically the family setting.

Joyce West Stevens provides further information about the connection between youths' search for validation and meaning-making. She asserts that adolescence is a period when young people embark upon a search for meaning and purpose in life. The importance of this search lies in the implications it has for developing decision-making skills and wisdom for facing the dilemmas of life.[4] She draws on the work of Fry, who underscores adolescent processes of meaning-making and forming wisdom or knowledge about important and difficult matters of life, ways of interpreting these matters, and the means of confronting the uncertainties, doubts, and choices.[5] Yet we can also see that youth may make choices that result in destructive forms of validation, as in Randy's choice of a gang as his alternative to the dearth of affirmation found at home.

SUFFERING ENGENDERED BY OPPRESSIVE CIRCUMSTANCES

Three of the four stories reflected youths' experiences of oppression. Michelle faced the oppression of church leaders because of their gender bias regarding the role of women guitarists. Rick found his home environment oppressive because of the injurious and vehement language directed toward him by his mother. Yvonne experienced her treatment at school as oppressive. In each case, the expressive manner in which the youth told the stories pointed to mental suffering or emotional hurt engendered by their experiences.

Adolescents' experiences of oppression heighten their sense of vulnerability and awareness of their limitations. These experiences also remind them of life's adversities. The challenge in adolescence is to develop a life-generating dynamic or spirituality that can make possible their ability to see life as valued and hopeful in spite of trials and tribulations.[6] Yet adolescents cannot do it alone.

Adolescents look to adults as guides and role models. When adults fail to act with integrity or when they act in ways that are wounding, they evoke in young people disappointment and expectations of negative behavior. Disappointment that leads to disillusionment can have frightening or tragic consequences in the lives of young people, as in cases of youth runaways and suicides. As young people become accustomed to the negative behavior of key adults in their lives, youth may also transfer their expectations of that behavior onto other adults, resulting in a nontrusting stance toward adults, or they may adopt that stance as their own. It is important to realize that the task in adolescence is one of assessing the behaviors of persons in their environment as means of reaching judgments about these behaviors and as part of the process of forming their own value system and setting their own goals.[7] Young people need guidance in engaging this process in helpful ways.

Stevens emphasizes that "moral agency is especially needed for undervalued youth coming of age in a hostile environment of ambiguous choices and relational estrangement. All youth as they mature along the life span must learn to develop the capacity to make commitments to personal goals *without* assurances of outcomes. This evolving capacity is a prime symptom of strength of character that is nourished by the construction of meaningful identities."[8] However, Stevens goes on to say that black youth have an added burden because of the presence of racism. They have an added task of developing "the capacity for care, nurturance, and oral commitments despite disempowering structural conditions that communicate a devalued self."[9] This task is not easy.

Based on what youth have to say, their peers internalize the negative attitudes and views of black people as well as stereotypical images portrayed on television and in movies, music, and videos. Their internalized view has emerged in what is called "thug life." A sixteen-year-old eleventh-grade student described the thug-life mentality in the following way: "Thug life is our aggression against the world. It is our way of being hard and fighting for our honor. . . . Hip-hop is our response to the oppression of African peoples." However, according to Bakari Kitwana, "Young Blacks have used this access both in pop film and music, far too much to strengthen associations between Blackness and poverty, while celebrating anti-intellectualism, ignorance, irresponsible parenting, and criminal lifestyles."[10] This is a paradox, given the growing influence of hip-hop. And, in the face of this growing popularity, we in our churches must come to grips with the fact that this new culture is an outgrowth of the conditions of our time. Our youth are completely submerged in it.

RESILIENCE

We must neither underestimate the resilience of black youth nor must we fail to identify it, promote it, and support it. By *resilience* is meant "the demonstration of hardiness, a focused commitment to follow events through, and a strong sense of self-efficacy."[11] In the earlier mentioned story, Michelle and her peers showed great resilience in their effort to forge a place for youth leadership and a positive response to gender bias. In the midst of Rick's deep disappointment, he acknowledged his gift of speaking and communicating his dream of a vocation in which this gift could be used. Even though Yvonne's hope for her selection for the international trip was not realized because of the school's rejection of her, she was able to renew a sense of hopefulness that she articulated with the words "I'm not going to give up." However, Stevens makes clear that youth need "support resources that serve as shock absorbers."[12]

Further Commentary on the Stories

In brief, what more do the stories tell us about black teen life? Michelle's story reveals a problematic issue in the life of congregations. Congregations cannot involve youth if we do not see them or honor them as valuable contributors and present-day leaders.

Congregations must be aware that our youth have a need to be recognized, validated, and appreciated. Black youth are cognizant of their need to exercise their spiritual gifts and talents. Many times they are denied opportunities to use those gifts and talents within congregational life. Churches must respond to this need or risk losing them entirely.

The need for positive affirmation not simply from congregation but also from family appeared dominantly in Rick's and Randy's stories. All too often the business of adult lives precludes them from seeing, hearing, or knowing the impact they have on the lives of their children. Some parents even doubt the impact they actually have on their teens because of their false assumption that the youths' peer group constitutes the primary source of influence. Even though there is a natural movement of adolescents from dependence to independence, youth continue to look to parents as a source of help, not hindrance.

The creation of support systems that will be the "shock absorber" and legitimize the personhood of youth as well as promote their positive interaction within the family, church, and community is critical. Particularly with regard to existing problems and conflicts in family contexts, it can be said that an important task of support systems within the church is to assist in what Blake Neff calls "the development of shared meanings between young people and their parents. That is, to assist in the improvement of communication between these two generational groups."[13] As indicated in the prologue, we are discovering that the need for support and even the education of parents is essential today because the larger communal or "village" support network has all but disappeared and parents are "out there" alone in the task of child-rearing.

Building on the stories, the themes in them, and our further commentary on them, we will explore a theology of presence, attentiveness, and compassion. Our purpose for this theological exploration is to provide foundational components for proposing a paradigm of advocacy and strategic action on behalf of black youth.

Discovery Through Theological Reflection

In order to meet the current-day challenge of seeing, hearing, and responding to our youth, we must have in mind a framework that guides us in how to do it. Such a framework must center on three primary theological ideas: presence, attentiveness, and compassion. A theology that incorporates these ideas will begin with a scriptural story, namely, the parable of the prodigal son. The use of this story is to provide a prism for looking at the situation of black teens today and those who nurture them.

In Jesus' parable of the prodigal son three aspects—presence, attentiveness, and compassion—emerge as powerful means of restoration, forgiveness, and identity validation for young persons moving through the transition of life. The prodigal son had issues with identity formation and personhood that took the form of what may be called adolescent rebellion. He defied the traditional norms of the inheritance being passed down through the generational sibling order. At a father's death, Jewish law allotted one-third of the estate to the younger son and two-thirds to the elder son (Deuteronomy 21:17). In this parable the younger son approached the father before the older brother and asked for his inheritance. The father did not rebuff him. Rather, he became wholly present to him. He showed attentiveness to his younger son's request; and out of awareness of the historical significance of the request, he granted to both sons his livelihood (Luke 15:12).

The prodigal son then exercised his desire for independence and self-encounter by traveling to a "far country," even though his journey promised questionable future life chances, suffering, and dwindling resources. Although the younger son's request portrayed his rebellious nature, the father supported his decision and waited patiently for the outcome. Lamenting his ultimate decision, the father did not force his will upon his son. Rather, he supported his son and loved him in spite of the circumstances. Based on the father's response at the end of the story, we may assume that throughout the whole experience of his son, the father's attention remained on his child. The role taken by the father was likely that of the waiting parent—a presence to the son even in the child's absence and an attentiveness to the needs of the son for welcome without judgment or retaliation.

In the midst of the father's presence and attentiveness at a distance, God moved on the heart of the youth. After losing all he had and experiencing the messiness of a hog pen, the son remembered his father's love (Luke 15:18). As part of his coming to a new awareness of self, the son entered into a period of reflection and questioning: "How many of my father's hired hands have bread enough and to spare, but here I am dying of hunger! I will get up and go to my father, and I will say to him, 'Father, I have sinned against heaven and before you; I am no longer worthy to be called your son; treat me like one of your hired hands.' So he set off and went to his father" (Luke 15:17-20*a*).

The father became the compassionate one who, when the son "came to himself" and appeared on the horizon, ran out to him, put his arms around him and kissed him (Luke 15:20*b*). The father said to the servants: "Quickly, bring out a robe—the best one—and put it on him; put a ring on his finger and sandals on his feet. And get the fatted calf and kill it, and let us eat and celebrate; for this son of mine was dead and is alive again; he was lost and is found! And they began to celebrate" (Luke 15:22-24). The presence, attentiveness, and compassion of the father brought about the son's recognition of his valued self.

The Prodigal Son's Story as a Matter of Discovery

Typically, attention is focused on the prodigal son, his rebellious journey away from home, and his return from the "far country." We discover in the story important insights about youth in general that go beyond the stories presented earlier in this chapter. The prodigal son reminds parents of a child's insistent statement, "It's mine! Give it to me!"[14] Youth today often couch this statement according to the material-oriented values of our society. They demand a car, or demand to drive, or demand particular kinds of clothes to wear. Like the prodigal son, youth today are apt to quickly demand their rights before they are fully cognizant of what is involved in caring fully for relationships. Likewise, the "far country's" appeal to the prodigal son may be likened to the yen of youth today to grow up fast and move away from home, or to successfully negotiate the extension of curfew to later and later hours, or to choose to enter into reckless behavior beyond their parents' or guardians' presence.

But the attitude and action of the prodigal son's father holds critical insights for a "real" Christian ministry. We find in the father keys to responding to black youths' search for identity validation, autonomy, and individuation; experiences of suffering; and show of resilience that must lead to positive ends. The father expresses a deeply felt love; and this love makes possible his presence, attentiveness, and compassion. This example is an essential requirement in "real" ministry with youth today. Black youth desperately need congregational leaders, members, and parents who are present to them, attentive to them, and compassionate toward them. Being "real" means demonstrating these qualities in the whole life of the church and providing guidance and support to assure the expression of these same qualities by the parents or guardians of the youth.

A commentator on the story of the prodigal son reminds us that the temptation adults face is to withdraw from youth in the midst of the youths' struggle for separation and need to forge their own unique identities. Succumbing to this temptation is tantamount to responding in kind.[15] Moreover, it may be all too easy for adults to discount youths' suffering in the fray of dealing with their own. And adults may mistakenly interpret the resilience of youth for impudence. But what we glean from the role of the father in the parable of the prodigal son is the reminder that, in every circumstance, our youth *are* our youth. We are reminded, too, of the necessity of our love for our youth that makes possible our presence, attentiveness, and compassion. Indeed, in this way we reflect God's love, and model for our youth a life-generating spirituality.

Toward Keeping It Real: A Paradigm of Advocacy and Strategic Action

This chapter began with the appeal of youth for the Christian community to "step up and take notice." It continued with the real stories of youth that demonstrate the veracity of this appeal. We have discovered the importance of our presence with our youth, attentiveness to them, and our compassion for them. What is needed to move from these discoveries to a live response? We want to propose three movements: First, we want to suggest that a start is to get in touch with the woundedness of our youth and to enter into a communal lament through which we "make real" our presence and attentiveness. Second, we will recommend ways of modeling compassion. Finally, we will set forth a list of concrete actions to be undertaken by the "village" with and on behalf of black youth.

Engaging and Moving Beyond Lament

The lament of the black Christian faith community begins with hearing youths' stories of struggle and suffering, and our feeling deeply their woundedness to the point that, like the father of the prodigal son, we run toward the youth and embrace them.[16] Entering into and moving beyond lament requires that we know the youths' stories and become co-present *with* them and attentive to them in the presence of God.[17] Co-presence denotes an intentionality in "being there" with our whole selves with the youth. We are physically near. Our focus is on them. To be attentive means being consciously aware of both the right and the need of youth to "tell it like it is," to question and complain to God and us—Doesn't God care? Don't you care? Attentiveness also means being ready for and supportive of the youths' expression of emotion such as weeping, wailing, and anger.[18] And attentiveness extends to an awareness of our own feelings, blame, and needs for change.

Ultimately, lament must lead to the adults' and youths' co-yearning before God for a new reality that differs from the present one.[19] The attentive role of adults in follow-up is to be in a constant state of readiness for supportive action on behalf of the youth. It means being consciously aware of the circumstances of our youth and being ready to work through whatever these circumstances are in a supportive way in recognition that black youth need a continuous level of support. In military circles, the command for attention means to assume the position, with heels together, body erect, arms at the side, and eyes to the front. Attentiveness in "real" youth ministry means that the community is positioned to provide stability, guidance, and leadership for our youth.

Modeling Compassion

Compassion is sometimes viewed as mere sympathy. *Webster's Collegiate Dictionary* indicates that compassion is "to sympathize; sympathetic consciousness of others' distress, together with a desire to alleviate it."[20] However, a deeper level of compassion is needed in order to address and make a difference in the lives of black youth. The community must exhibit the kind of compassion that God displays for God's people. We must model the kind of compassion that the father of the prodigal son showed toward him. We must model the kind of compassion that Jesus consistently demonstrated for persons in need—an unconditional love that derives from the root word *compassio*, which means "to suffer with."

The book *The Black Church in the African American Experience* describes the black church as an institution that "is struggling for relevance in the resolution of today's black problems."[21] There is a tendency of our churches not wanting to get our shirts dirty. But ministry with youth that "keeps it real" requires at times our "getting in the hog pen with them." Or, as the youth exclaim, it means feeling what they feel, experiencing their pain, seeing them, hearing them, and engaging them, if we're going to win them.

We cannot afford to be turned off by their lifestyles, irritated by their dress codes, oblivious to their culture, or threatened by their giftedness. These *are* our children. We *must* embrace every aspect of who they are in order to nurture them into what God has created them to be. Moreover, we are reminded that "providing this care cannot happen without the faith community's awareness of black youths' empowerment or sense of agency to survive and thrive in an alienating, violent, and wounding world."[22] Compassionate care rests on the community's being a holding environment where youth can experience solace and renewal, guidance and sustenance, and a belief system that makes possible their formation of hope as well as their ability to recover from adversity.[23] A compassionate community must provide for black youth a place and a ministry where bonding and solidarity are authentically experienced.[24]

A List of Concrete Actions

The youth hope-building model carried out in the Youth Hope-Builders Academy has experienced a great deal of success. This success can be attributed to the kinds of advocacy and strategic action that empowers adults' co-action with black youth. If congregations accept the challenge to see, hear, and engage youth—indeed, to be present, attentive, and compassionate—then we must have a plan of action. A strategic action plan necessarily answers the questions *What can we do? What is our far-reaching vision? What are we hoping to accomplish?* The following are eight key components of the youth hope-building model that draws from an African-centered ideal of building and sustaining "the village." An old African proverb states, "It takes a village to raise a child." It further states that "it takes a village to sustain a village."[25]

1. Recognize the tremendous stake we have in the nurture and survival of our youth. They have an innate need to be recognized, validated, and given guidance in order to grow and mature as positive agents in the church and world. It takes the entire "village" to make this a reality.
2. Acknowledge our faith communities as imperative locations for conversation with youth and information sharing. The model of the Youth Hope-Builders Academy includes the sponsorship of an annual community-wide youth and family convocation and additional forums that identify and address pertinent issues facing youth, their families, and the larger "village" today.
3. Be proactive in providing and modeling values and commitments for youth to emulate. The overwhelming theme in the cry of our youth is, Why are adults so hypocritical in their portrayal of Christian values? Adult mentors and others who provide leadership in the Youth Hope-Builders Academy model character and consistency in their relationship with the Creator. The Christian lifestyle must be perceived as authentic by our youth if we're going to reach them.
4. Recognize the tremendous stake we have in engaging our youth in congregational ministry efforts. Black teens understand that ministry is a part of their lives. They want to engage in ministry. Provide them with opportunities to express themselves as they choose. The Youth Hope-Builders Academy model allows the teens to serve on the advisory board and to provide leadership in the development of curriculum, recreational activities, praise and worship services, and serving as peer mentors. The youth lead worship through dance, mime, rap, stepping, spoken word, and Scripture reading. Youth must feel the freedom to have perfect self-expression.
5. Make a commitment to patience and persistence in working with young people. Consistent and effective follow-up is needed to sustain progress. Taking the advocates' role requires

continuous oversight in their lives. The Youth Hope-Builders Academy model provides consistent feedback and the maintenance of a database that tracks every youth that matriculates through the program. Mentors provide continual guidance and nurture. The quarterly forums give opportunity for communication and relationship re-formation. It is important never to lose touch with our youth.

6. Stand united in placing our youths' needs higher than our own interests. The mantra of the Youth Hope-Builders Academy model is "We must do more." We will never become complacent or satisfied with what we have accomplished. We continue to duplicate and expand on what we are doing. Sharing what we do with others is integral to "real" youth ministry in order that others can see and use what is applicable for their ministries.

7. Create a sense of global perspective for black youth. Technology has created a global world. Our youth need to recognize their place and role in that united yet often troublesome world. The Youth Hope-Builders Academy model provides video-conferencing with youth in South Africa and Bermuda and exposes youth to information given by speakers from the international community. Bringing together African American youth, and black youth from Africa, the Caribbean, Bermuda, and other parts of the world helps all of them to affirm the Pan-African "village" and to honor the similarities and uniqueness of members of this "village."

8. Finally, contribute to our youths' self-confidence, self-reliance, resilience, courage, and vocational direction by exposing them to biblical and cultural history. The Youth Hope-Builders Academy model teaches identity and relationship to the African American cultural heritage through cultural field trips, readings, role-play, and simulations. Exploration of a broad range of Christian vocations occurs through speakers, the completion of gifts inventories, and small-group dialogue. Self, cultural, community, and Christian identity develops through a wide range of exposures.

Another African proverb says, "I am because you are." It is an expression of groupness, sameness in the midst of uniqueness, cooperation, and responsibility. African philosopher John Mbiti defines African philosophy as the understanding; attitude of mind; logic; and perception behind the manner in which African people think, act, feel, or speak in different situations of life.[26] Central to Mbiti's definition is the "spiritual disposition," "collective consciousness," or kind of "*vita* attitude" or life orientation that reflects faith in a transcendental force and a sense of vital solidarity.[27] This view has relevance for our way toward "keeping it real."

In addition to the eight key components mentioned above, it is important to add that black youth have an innate need to honor the Creator of life. There is no empowerment, growth, or transformation without recognition and appreciation for the transcendental force present in all life forms. Black youth need guidance on how to effectively commune with and develop a relationship with God. The importance of this is three-fold: (1) Youth gain an awareness of God's value of them, and God's love reflected in the response of the waiting parent in the parable of the prodigal son; (2) youth come to realize that there is a Power greater than themselves to which they are accountable; and (3) they can appreciate having that One whom they can call on, cry out to, and trust unconditionally, knowing that this Holy One's presence, attentiveness, and compassion does not fail. An important manner in which adults guide youth toward a relationship with God is through modeling our own relationship with God and through our laying bare the depth of this relationship in our own expression of presence, attentiveness, and compassion with our youth.

Questions for Reflection and Discussion

1. What are some of the stories the youth around you have shared?
2. What are the youths' needs for presence, attentiveness, and compassion from adults in your congregation?
3. What are the adults' needs for presence, attentiveness, and compassion? To whom do they turn for these needs to be met?
4. How could you make the paradigm of advocacy and strategic action come alive in your congregation, family, or community?

It is important to note that although black youth are energetic and extremely gifted, they experience a great deal of anxiety. This anxiety sometimes results in their reticence to engage in a lot of discussion about their aversions. But they want and need to share their stories and must be invited to do so in a safe environment with trusted adults. We, as congregational leaders and adults in families and communities, must answer the call to see them, hear them, and engage them lest we lose them.

CHAPTER 3

Getting Real

Maisha I. Handy and Daniel O. Black

Talking with one another is loving one another.

—A Kenyan proverb

Introduction

As a young person growing up in a Baptist church, I had a phenomenal youth minister. Reverend Frances was vibrant and enthusiastic, always ready to engage youth. Our interest in Sunday school and Baptist Training Union classes was beginning to wane when she was assigned to meet with us weekly. I specifically remember a Sunday evening when Reverend Frances decided to create a youth talk show. Rather than follow the preselected, predetermined curriculum, she used her creativity as a way of meeting us where we were as black youth spiritually, emotionally, and developmentally. She selected two talk-show hosts from the youth group and arranged the rest of us as the audience. We traversed topics that were relevant to our real-lived experiences. We were invited to speak from our self-understanding and experiences up to that point of our young lives, bringing spiritual principles to bear upon our dialogue. No topic was taboo. Nothing was too sacred to touch. We were, in two words, "getting real."

As indicated in the prologue, bringing "real-ness" to youth ministry means placing at the center the concrete life experiences and concerns of youth and inviting honest exploration of them.[1] This kind of ministry focuses on honest and forthright engagement of youth with adults who exemplify a genuine real-ness for youth to imitate. It was this quality of self and approach to youth ministry that Reverend Frances demonstrated.

The need for genuine and transparent teachers of youth is more essential today than ever before in our history as black people. Cornel West characterizes our culture today as one in which there is a loss of love, a loss of meaning, and a loss of purpose.[2] Historically, our churches and civic institutions helped us to become full human beings despite what was going on in wider culture. Formerly, our churches were the places where everyone could go to feel a sense of welcome, hospitality, and love. Today, however, there are market forces and market moralities that are undermining the connectional roots of the black church, according to West.[3] West concludes that market-driven forces are destroying black families, neighborhoods, schools, churches, and mosques. As a result, black people are more vulnerable and fragile in our daily lives.[4]

The fracturing of the church and institutions of the black community due to market driven forces is felt severely by our black youth. Some black churches seem captured by these market-driven forces, and our youth are feeling the devastating impact of this captivity. Years ago when black churches in the South were being burned, many churches would have been shocked if black youth were the culprits. Is it conceivable that black children are so disgusted with the only institution their parents govern that, instead of perpetuating it against their will, they would rather destroy it? Why? Because instead of building beloved communities, the church seems to be perpetuating exclusive clubs in which only certain people are allowed and where youth are largely silenced. The church was conceived as a place where anyone is welcome, black youth are told, but the rejection of certain members of the population make young people question whether God is really the head of the church. Young people want a place—unlike schools, nightclubs, and malls—where they don't have to live exclusively according to market standards in order to be embraced. They want a place where differences don't divide, where character and kindness rule, where adults love more than ridicule. They don't want to be evaluated by market-driven values that reduce worth to commodities to be bought and sold based on power, wealth, prestige, beauty, and popularity. The fact that many churches have not met this need to belong and to be unconditionally accepted is undoubtedly frustrating to youth, especially since they have nowhere else to turn. The hope for a beloved community is quickly dwindling into disappointment in an institution that promised salvation to all.

Given the current context of marketing forces affecting the lives of our black youth, and the relative impotence of the church to respond, black youth are left floundering without compass or rudder. Thus, youth are raising serious questions about the viability of the church for connecting with their lives. This is particularly critical when they are struggling with such issues as suicide; homosexuality; sexual intercourse and oral sex; and violence. In addition, incest in many homes and older people seeking youth as sex partners even within the church are issues that demand church attention. These realities exist among youth today, but the youth are not finding an openness to discuss these concerns in churches. They view the church as silent on these issues and thus feel rejected. The question is, How can we help this current generation of young Christians carry out their faith formation while facing these real-life issues? It is critical that the church not only address the real issues facing our youth but also provide a safe environment where "real" ministry with youth can take place. This environment is where youth can be real and can expect adults to be genuine and transparent with them.

This chapter seeks to outline and address problems and tensions existing between youth and congregations and to offer some approaches for "real" ministry. The chapter recognizes that certain things can be accomplished in public worship to make youth feel at home and welcomed, but it also recognizes that there are other settings that provide safety and confidentiality for youth to reveal their real concerns and issues. The basic position here is that the church must provide safe and caring environments where youth can be vulnerable and feel their experiences will neither be discounted nor exploited.

Can I Get a Mentor?

How often do we hear complaints about "these crazy young people" when a youth is acting outside what we deem to be normative and acceptable behavior? Youth endure a constant barrage of criticism related to their clothing, behavior, topics of interest, music, and other cultural expressions. Often, the critique comes without any meaningful dialogue *with* youth about who they are and how and why they make choices.

Proverbs 22:6 states, "Train children in the right way, and when old, they will not stray." In this verse, training has often been misinterpreted to mean that forceful lecturing or corporal punishment should be the approach to prepare children for right or principled life. In contrast, it should be interpreted as taking time needed to instruct, communicate with, and guide a child into responsible living. This kind of preparation is at the heart of mentoring. Yet, *mentoring* has become a profane word in many pockets of the black community. Our youth need wisdom, counsel, and nurture that come from wise adults who are willing to commit to being involved in the lives of youth on a consistent basis.

Why are so many adults and churches averse to mentoring programs? Perhaps the answer lies in the ways in which living in a capitalist, consumer culture with all its commitments prevents most Americans from having much time for meaningful and sustained interactions with others, including their children. Or, is it the deeply rooted individualism that disrupts black family life, communal life, and village consciousness? Maybe adults are simply tired and have given up. The constraints of contemporary American life have created an entire generation that has been raised by television. Some blame the black matriarch, claiming that she is insufficient for the task of raising her children alone, especially male children. But from a historical perspective, Wade Nobles reminds us, "What is important to understand, in this society particularly, is that what has been critical in black families is not whether it's female-headed or male-headed, but whether the *survival of the tribe* (family) was maintained."[5]

Mentoring might also be objectionable to black adults because of the level of vulnerability it requires. Said differently, the survival motif among African Americans has often been to "suck up" hurt and get over it or "turn burdens over to the Lord" instead of facing them for oneself. Consequently, the historical precedent established has been for black folk not to expose their hurting hearts either to the world or to one another. However, effective mentoring requires such exposure—especially with angry, frustrated young people—rather than adults' tendency toward superficial forms of relating that disallow youths' "disturbance" of the walls of protection enclosing adults' fragile hearts. Blatantly stated, the childhood horrors of many black adults hinder their ability to employ mentoring as a viable tool in the transformation of black youth. Traumatic events and questionable outcomes of the Civil Rights Movement, the disillusioning sentiment of "Black Power," and beating and verbal abuse in child-rearing practices in black families have left many black adults today so privately pained that their interpersonal skills appear dysfunctional.

So, in far too many instances, the unfortunate answer to the question of black youth, "Can I get a mentor?" is "No" because parents and their peers are so fragile internally as to be ashamed of what the youth would discover if they let them get too close. For example, the facade of strength and courage of some adults would crumble like a sand castle in the wind if youth were to ask them to revisit their relationship with their own parents or to explain why they don't touch them and tell them they're beautiful. Put simply, until black churches facilitate the healing of black adults—the kind of healing that can take place, for example, by replacing the Sunday morning sermon with one-on-one sharing time—many black children will remain at arm's distance from their elders.

Truthfully, more is needed than the present makeshift forms of youth ministry such as pointless youth Bible studies from a prescribed curriculum, lock-ins where youth are either talked at or talk only to each other all night long, or laughable Youth Day programs that celebrate and situate young people in the center of our churches once a year. Our youth are crying out for more than what they describe as useless, ineffective Sunday school classes where critical life questions and topics they confront are considered taboo and are therefore ignored. They want more than the approaches to youth ministry that are considered by them to be a waste of time. There is a desperate cry of our young for real connection to the black church, its leaders, and its adult members. In far too many instances, it can be said that we are sending mixed messages and our children have found us out. They know what they need and they know that we can't—or won't face our own demons—to provide it. In many instances, the black church has become a joke to black youth.

Undoubtedly, the most scathing criticism leveled against the black church by its youth is the blatant hypocrisy they witness. On any given Sunday, young people watch adults raise their hands in praise, speak in unknown tongues, dance the aisles, cry a river, but after the thrill is gone, adult behavior is often inconsistent with such spiritual ecstasy. The youth do not make sense of the double standard shown in "churchly" behavior on the one hand, and the use of hurtful and profane language on the other hand. Youth raise questions about what they see as unchristian attitudes and the unequal roles of males and females in church leadership. These inconsistencies cause black youth to question the integrity of black church worship, congregational life, and the Christian life. Often they conclude that shouting and crying are a hoax. They ask, "What is all the drama for?" "Why does the Holy Ghost only seem to make adults better during church services?" Who can blame them? They think that spiritual ecstasy is supposed to result in transformed adults who love beyond preferences and who take the chance to give of themselves until it hurts. They conclude that if the Holy Ghost can't transform people's everyday lives, then they don't want the Holy Ghost.

Our youth want to see adults live the faith they shout about. And, for them, this living becomes evident in a church that functions as a village—where adults welcome them, love them, listen to them, guide them, and apologize when they as adults fall short of what they said they would do. And they want parents who do likewise. Our youth want—in fact require—healthy mentoring relationships with adults who model consistency in living the faith they espouse. They want and require "real" ministry provided by mature, genuine adults who do not relegate them to places of silence and invisibility but whose interest is in our youths' surviving and thriving in today's and tomorrow's world.

Village functions must be recovered if our youth are to thrive spiritually, emotionally, psychologically, and relationally.[6] This village recognizes that mentoring is not simply linear or one-way, but circular. Youth are mentored by adults, but at times youth tutor or teach adults about issues pertinent to contemporary life. For example, youth can teach adults about computer technology while simultaneously receiving wisdom about life from that same adult. Our village must strive to empower youths to reach their full potential. It must help youth claim their voices by respectfully raising critical questions and engaging in critical analysis in the midst of intergenerational fellowship and dialogue. In what follows, we will propose several approaches that are needed to carry out village functions, including an African-centered approach, nurturing youth into wholeness, fostering critical consciousness, and mentoring for meaningful praxis.

An African-centered Approach

The formation of a valued identity is of central importance to black youths' surviving and thriving. Our youth search for it and form it in their interactions with family, peers, communities of significance, and, in this era, through contact with mass media. Black congregations must be both aware of and willing to engage these circles of significance if they are to contribute to a positive sense of self and spiritual formation.

Retrieving African and African American History and Traditions

Retrieving our history and traditions is vital to the task of enabling and empowering black youth. Oppression and victimization suffered by black people have spawned decades of either resistance to or ignorance of African and African American history and culture. Jawanza Kunjufu asks, "[H]ow can you expect victims who have never been taught their history, or have only been taught it in February [Black History Month], or have only been given a docile approach to their history, to realize its importance? Most Black people end up saying, 'I don't want to hear that black stuff.'"[7]

There was a period during the 1970s and 1980s when African American churches moved toward the embrace of African culture and incorporated black images and artifacts in worship and architecture. Many took seriously African traditional rituals and ceremonies such as rites of passage as a way of expressing black identity. Unfortunately, much of it turned out to be a passing fad. We need to return to a more serious engagement of African traditions for what they have to offer for our recovery of village functions, particularly because taking village life for granted both here and in Africa is no longer possible.[8]

Although not all black churches today reject our unique cultural history, there is certainly a need for a wider embrace of cultural approaches to spirituality. Rites of passage programs in our churches are an important way of initiating these approaches and of carrying out the requirement of mentoring black youth. Employing these programs may mean overcoming false assumptions that they counter Christian convictions.[9] What may be needed, in fact, is the movement beyond positions of self-hatred espoused in statements such as "I ain't black, I'm saved!" or "My identity is in Christ!"—as though race becomes irrelevant when one becomes a Christian. The critical need is to move beyond black disdain for blackness, and the ease and willingness to drop our racial and cultural heritage in place of a supposedly divine—meaning white—Christian identity. To black youth, this self-rejection and concomitant embrace of a decidedly European self means that the church, like every other institution in America, is committed to the perpetuation of Eurocentric values demonstrated, for example, in obtaining money (prosperity teaching).

White images of Christ still hover over many black sanctuaries—no wonder, then, that black congregations often read the Bible through Eurocentric lens. The remedy to the problem is simply the belief that to be unapologetically African is not contrary to what it means to be Christian. At least, it's not supposed to be. For an oppressed people who have lived in a racist America for four hundred years or more, the need to read the Bible through African eyes is more critical than ever before.[10] The importance of this hermeneutical shift becomes dramatized in ways black youth express themselves and receive criticism for that expression. For example, black youth who choose African expressions through clothing and hairstyles are often chastised by adults. Because adults do not see that an attempt to love God without loving one's African self first is a contradiction, they have been known to confront black youth with statements such as "Do something with yo' nappy head befo' coming to the house of the Lord." Why God requires a particular hairstyle, of course, makes no sense to youth. But more important, the view that God doesn't like natural African hair is even more confusing. In the end, black youth either internalize these debilitating ideologies, or they abandon the church altogether and choose alternative frames of reference. More specifically, to the extent black churches disclaim their spirituality in terms of their own African heritage, youth will cleave to hip-hop and other popular forms in order to find some semblance of positive self-regard.

Village-building Processes

In her chapter on the importance of culture in wisdom formation, Yolanda Smith laments the appropriation of teaching methods and techniques that are not helpful for black youth. She expresses concern that "the uses of these approaches in black churches override adoption of rich sources of wisdom from the black oral tradition, such as music, dance, poetry, ritual, proverbs, metaphors, stories, and historical accounts."[11] Our resistance to or our ignoring our own traditions supports our inconsistency in teaching them. "Real" village-building for the sake of the youth requires that our communities and churches engage in "sankofa," which is built on an Akan symbol[12] and focused on reaching back and retrieving some of the rituals, relationality, and cultural vehicles and forms of our history—incorporating them into the everyday rituals of our lives.

At the same time, because of our youths' embrace of it, we must not shun hip-hop culture. Rather, we must find ways of embracing and integrating it with other cultural strands. The daily expressions of youth need to be included not only in what we teach but also in how we teach. Furthermore, we must be open to our own creativity and the inventive spirit of youth when planning and governing church services, church school classes, and Bible studies. A serious paradigm shift is needed both in our structure and method. The history and legacy of Africa, the African diaspora, and the journey of black people in this country from slavery forward must be at the center of any attempt to institutionalize intergenerational learning experiences that aim toward village-building and the practice of freedom.

What we are suggesting here also builds on the assertion of Cornel West some years ago that many black youth continue to wrestle with "nihilism," or sense of meaninglessness, purposelessness, and love-lessness.[13] As youth teeter on the edge of hopelessness and identity crises, it is imperative that churches and other communities of significance provide both the kind of structure that is representative of a consistently "real" community of care, and a space where they can openly express their fears, anxieties, and ambivalence.

In his book *The Healing Wisdom of Africa*, Malidoma Somé discusses the centrality of ritual in the community-building processes of indigenous societies. Somé contends that "the West is struggling with the loss of connection . . . and the ability to bring . . . needed healing."[14] As youth struggle with feelings of hopelessness, they are further discouraged by what they see as a disconnect among generations. The youth are gifted but have no place in which they can practice aligning their gifts with their life purpose. As Somé states, "Whether they are raised in indigenous or modern culture, there are two things that people crave: the full realization of their innate gifts, and to have these gifts approved, acknowledged, and confirmed."[15] The ritual life of the church provides both a place where gifts can be expressed and affirmed, and the necessary wisdom needed to help youths identify who they are and their purpose in God's plan. Somé states:

> Purpose begins with the individual, and the sum total of all the individuals' purposes creates the community's purpose. The community thus takes upon itself the responsibility of nurturing and protecting the individual, because the individual, knowing her or his purpose, will then invest energy in sustaining the community . . . the community recognizes that its own vitality is based in the support and protection of each of its individuals, especially in the constant support and reminding of each individual of his or her purpose. The individual, knowing this, in turn delivers to the community the gifts that the community has successfully awakened in him or her.[16]

The church community is a village of affirmation and support through reciprocity. The nurturing, guiding, sustaining function of this village is distinctly carried out through ritual practice, and "ritual is an art, an art that weaves and dances with symbols, and helping to create that art rejuvenates participants."[17]

According to Somé, "Ritual is central to village life, for it provides the focus and energy that holds the community together, and . . . provides the kind of healing that the community most needs to survive."[18] A helpful approach to helping black youth to receive the healing they so desperately need is using the stories, proverbs, rites, and educational experiences of African heritage to highlight milestones in their development. These markers help to usher youth through major life changes. Rituals from birth to death are common, but, as Somé notes, "what is lacking in this rich life experience is a community that observes the individual's growth and certifies that one has passed through an initiatory process."[19]

We have already pointed to the importance of rites of passage. Here, we want to emphasize that the processes of initiation or rites of passage ensure that youth are not simply heard, but take responsibility for attaining knowledge and for giving back reciprocally to community. One example of a rites of passage program that integrates Christian doctrine in order to nurture black youth is found at Zion Baptist Church of Washington, D.C. This particular program is an extensive one for black boys. The initiates are guided through the mastery of key principles. They participate in several major rituals, including a naming ceremony. As Somé states, "Ritual provides not only healing but also the recovery of memory and reaffirmation of each individual's life purposes."[20] By affirming their birth names and adding an African name, initiates link with a tradition. The added names reflect the initiates' current character and the characteristics and purpose to which the community would like initiates to aspire. As a "crossing" or graduation journey and celebration, the initiates travel to Ghana, West Africa, venturing through Accra and Kamase to experience African history and culture firsthand.

One of the experiences of youth participants in the Youth Hope-Builders Academy, to which the last chapter refers, entails their firsthand worship experiences in an African congregation and in an Africentric African American congregation. Youth learn African ways of life and approaches to the Christian faith from African adults and peers. Moreover, they connect with stories of black people from slavery forward through visits to historic sites such as the Civil Rights Institute in Birmingham, Alabama, and the Martin Luther King Center for Social Change and King's birthplace in

Atlanta, Georgia. And they hear the wisdom of elders who have lived the faith in the midst of hard trials and tribulations.

The point here is that connecting the rich traditions of African and African American heritage with faith tradition is quite fruitful. Building and sustaining a sense of healthy identity and purposeful living in black youth necessitates a communal approach. Many black youth live in communities and family structures that are fragmented. With the absence of a parent and no extended family available, they negotiate the complexities of life with little assistance. Other youths are deeply connected to families, but they need a wider village of support. Additional support is needed to buttress the involvement and support of parents and immediate family members in the academic achievements, extracurricular activities, and church involvement of youth.

Intergenerational activities and ritual practices provide youth with the support and nurturing they need to navigate and negotiate the many twists and turns endemic to young lifestyles. We must counter the deformations that result from the imposition of Eurocentric culture and perspectives. We must affirm and embrace ourselves! Black youth need to know that they belong, they are heard, they have gifts, and they are beautiful. To the extent this happens, we sow our seriousness about "getting real."

Questions for Reflection and Discussion

1. When you think about the African continent, what images come to mind? Which African countries and cultures are you familiar with and/or have a desire to learn more about? How can understandings of Africa and African approaches to Christianity be incorporated into your church life?

2. How do African identity and culture affirm or detract from your Christian identity? Where is African history and presence found in the Bible?

Practical Exercises for "Getting Real"

Exercise 1

Give each youth a piece of paper and a pen. Invite the youth to write down every negative use of the color or term "black" they have ever encountered. Encourage them to explore magazine articles they may have read, movies they have seen, cultural expressions they have heard, and even biblical references that speak of "black" in a derogatory manner. Certainly the youth will think of a few such expressions; however, the youth leader should be prepared to show the youth the countless ways whereby blackness is demeaned in American culture and how the result has often led to black self-hatred and self-rejection. Examples include "devil's (black) food cake vs. angel's (white) food cake"; "the black sheep of the family"; "Black Friday"; "nasty black licorice"; and "If you're white, you're all right; if you're black, get back." Examples like these must be examined for how they reinforce white supremacy and, indeed, prepare black youth to embrace a white God. This exercise also begs black youth leaders to investigate the extent to which their youth embrace a white image of Christ and what the ramifications of such embracing might be.

Exercise 2

In this exercise, ask the youth to act out what they imagine to be a day in the life of an African village. Adults can provide no instructions or guidance concerning what youth should do. The youth should act out whatever they think Africans do on an average, daily basis. Youth leaders can specify a particular country if they think youth would be more familiar with it; otherwise, let the youth act out their perceptions. Watch for the display of gender roles, cultural/religious beliefs, parent-child relationships, and so forth. More than likely, stereotypes will govern the performance as the youth expose various perceptions of Africa typically gathered from popular media sources. This exercise is an excellent way of helping youth understand how perceptions of people shape our assumptions about them and their spirituality. For example, understanding Africa as a land of pagans and heathens necessarily leads to black self-hatred and denunciation of an African spiritual legacy.

Follow up with information by African writers about an African country. Bring cultural artifacts, pictures, music, videos, and so forth. Use these items to counter stereotypes about monolithic, non-dynamic African communities. Seek the input and stories from Africans in your congregation or community and engage in conversations with them about their experiences with and images of African Americans. Focus on what Africans and African Americans can learn together.

Nurturing Youth into Wholeness: A Communicative Approach

Black youth struggle for wholeness or a positive sense of the spiritual, emotional, psychological, and relational self in community. But one of the most difficult impediments to moving through this struggle has to do with both the church's and parents'/guardians' reticence to "get real" about what may be called taboo topics. Churches and parents/guardians alike have largely missed the boat especially regarding sexuality and youth as sexual beings. As a result, youth are often left adrift to find their own answers and draw their own conclusions to questions about sexual identity, drive, and activity. Undertaking "real" youth ministry means providing opportunities with the guidance of expert counselors that help parents/guardians know how to engage their children on the topic of spirituality and sexuality and that engage youth with the permission of parents in the same. This engagement will necessarily focus on:

- solitary sex experiences of youth in their sleep, in their fantasy, and through masturbation;
- interpersonal sex, including topics ranging from petting to premarital sex, oral sex, anal sex, protected sex, and abstinence;
- homosexual orientation, behavior, and lifestyle;
- teenage pregnancy, abortion, and teen parenthood;
- sexually transmitted diseases (STDs) and HIV/AIDS; and
- sexual abuse.

Attention also needs to be given to the influence of the media through which youth "are exposed to a variety of ideologies, lifestyles and value systems that promote a freewheeling, overpermissive approach to sex."[21] In fact, research reported by Harley Atkinson shows that "two of the primary sources of information about sex for churched youth are media: movies and television. This means the media are providing sexual training for a large proportion of youth."[22] At the same time, it is also crucial to give focused thought to the values and norms communicated and lived by parents/guardians, other adults in the lives of youth, and peers, and to extend our outreach to youth and their parents/guardians beyond our congregations. Three sources that provide helpful overviews of sexuality in adolescence are Atkinson's chapter entitled "The Maze of Teenage Sexuality" in his book *Ministry with Youth in Crisis;*[23] *The Handbook of Youth Ministry,* by Donald Ratliff and James A. Davies;[24] and Joyce West Stevens' discussion on "Dealing with Having Sex" in her book *Smart and Sassy: The Strengths of Inner-city Black Girls.*[25]

Of course the topic of sexuality is not the only one that is left out of ministry with today's youth. In order to be "real," this ministry must engage youth in conversations that broach everything they face in their everyday lives, such as faith and health, racism, education, jobs, derogatory language, materialism, and patriarchy. The plight of black youth demands that we come out of our comfort zones, embrace our children, and address their quest for healing and hope as well as our own. It means that we also recognize the gifts and talents of our youth and their desire to share them in congregational life. Youth want to be whole! Black communal life must provide nurture that contributes to their physical, psychological, and spiritual development. We take on the important task of nurture through having dialogue, exploring what constitutes healthy self-image and living, promoting youth leadership and gift-sharing, and giving overall purposeful attention to the whole realm of identity formation and affirmation. Doing so also requires the recognition that the nurturing process is *work.* It is time-consuming and insists upon a level of vulnerability from everyone involved. It also means that, at times, youth themselves are not always willing to engage in all that the process entails. In such moments, youth leaders are simply called to continue as wholly present caring guides.

Questions for Reflection and Discussion

1. What is your understanding of nurturing? Whose job is it to provide it?
2. With what African rites of passage or mentoring programs are you familiar? How may such programs be helpful in the nurture and development of youth in your church and community?

3. As a pastor, youth minister, or parent/guardian, to what extent is dialogue a central part of your interactions with youth? To what extent is it central to your church community life?

A Practical Exercise for "Getting Real"

During a lesson on gifts, call out certain gifts and talents and ask the youth who have these gifts to share some of them in the group setting. Call out the following categories:

- Singer
- Comedian
- Poet
- Instrumentalist
- Artist
- Add your own categories

Use these demonstrations as opportunities to teach support and affirmation among youth.

Think! Fostering Critical Consciousness in Black Youth

In his seminal work entitled *Education for Critical Consciousness*, Paulo Freire reminds us that "human beings are active beings, capable of reflection on themselves and on the activity in which they are engaged. They are able to detach themselves from the world in order to find their place in it and with it. Only people are capable of this act of 'separation' in order to find their place in the world and enter in a critical way into their own reality. 'To enter into' reality means to look at it objectively, and apprehend it as one's field of action and reflection."[26]

While all humans are capable of this kind of evaluation, Freire highlights the need for a heightened level of evaluation and assessment that he calls "critical consciousness." Critical consciousness is defined as reaching a state of critical awareness that enables a person to both perceive and act upon their world in ways that bring forth transformation.

Freire warns against what he calls "massification" (the choice to follow the dominant group) and "simplism" (a pattern of thought that reduces the answer to every problem to a simple binary choice).[27] Youth in general, and black youth in specific, are often in a paradoxical position. Postmodern youth often resist the practice of blindly following doctrines, cultural norms, and authority without any critical assessment. And yet when it comes to their own peer groups, cultural norms, and preferences, assessment and evaluation can be difficult. Developing a sense of critical awareness can help youth to analyze their world and filter out those things that do not contribute to healthy identity and life practices.

Youth today are inundated with norms and values that contradict their faith. As American youth, they are entrenched in individualistic, self-centered, and self-serving values and motives; and they are socialized in ways that desensitize them to greed, violence, and abuse. Tom Beaudoin reminds us that even the seemingly most irreverent youth are on a spiritual quest, but many of them have become disenchanted by institutionalized religions that make no room beyond traditional dogma. He further asserts that we may be missing a prophetic voice by refusing to hear the critical analysis of youth found in their music, dance, poems, and direct expressions of critique of the church.[28] They need an ongoing forum at home, school, and church that challenges them to reflect upon and critique culture.

It is quite alarming how few Americans in general, and black youth in specific, are unable to engage in critical dialogue and analysis. Whether it is politics, theology, or even a movie, many along with the adults around them are locked into dichotomous thinking that does not allow for dialogue on complex issues, or we choose not to think at all. Youth are clearly affected by and concerned about both their immediate and the wider world, but they often lack the kind of self-actualization necessary for employing critical consciousness. It is also the case that they have brilliant thoughts and ideas that are silenced.

If the church plans to address the social ills plaguing its members, including the massive flight of youth and young adults away from primarily mainline churches, it must be willing to change its approach. Churches need to recognize the quest of all human beings for liberation from what is life-negating to a sense of human wholeness; and they seek "conscientization" or a level of awakening or critical awareness that leads to liberation.[29] This can occur only through critical educational effort. If education is the practice of freedom, then work with black youth must include mentoring youth into critical awareness. Sitting in a sterile classroom environment where lecturing from predetermined curriculum topics occurs is antithetical to the task of engaging youth in liberative praxis. We must be willing to "hear into speech" the values and concerns of younger generations—guiding them in the decision-making processes that enable them to be transforming agents in the world. Freire states: "Humans find themselves marked by the results of their own actions in their relations with the world, and through their action on it. By acting they transform; by transforming they create a reality which conditions their manner of acting. Thus it is impossible to dichotomize human beings and the world, since the one cannot exist without the other."[30]

When we decide to engage in honest meaningful dialogue with black youth, we involve ourselves in the task of engendering the critical thinking skills they need to decipher and navigate their world and the larger world of which they are part. We also help them realize that they have within themselves creative power to move beyond the hopelessness to which we referred earlier. We help them claim their abilities to move beyond simply identifying problems. They become agents of change, bringing into fruition the components of a world where they can reach their greatest potential.

Central to answering the clarion call of engendering critical consciousness, then, is the need to empower young people to claim their own gifts, wisdom, and abilities. In other words, we must do the true work of a guide, which is not to give all of the answers but to help the seeker to discover the truths within. This suggests a paradigm shift that places youth at the center of "real" youth ministry and curriculum. The Sunday morning worship is often not long enough or diverse enough to single-handedly address youth issues and foster their leadership skills. Why not begin sessions with youth outside worship that begin with open, honest questions about critical issues and that challenge youth to articulate their own views? Why not bring in sources that they read, and engage youth beyond the Bible and church-school curriculum as a way of discussing their cultural elements? This kind of shift in method models the very liberation that churches seek and youth need. It counteracts passive learning and invites youth to be active participants in constructing meaningful responses to community concerns.

Questions for Reflection and Discussion

1. To what extent does the theology of your church support raising questions? To what extent are sources beyond the Bible engaged? What sources beyond the Bible are read and explored? What attitudes exist in your church about readings beyond the Bible?

2. To what degree are youth utilized in every Sunday morning service? In what ways do youth interact with church officials or leaders within and beyond the confines of the church? What interactions take place between the youth and the clergy?

3. What willingness do church adults exhibit to listen to hip-hop music? How would you describe their level of willingness to listen to enough hip-hop music to engage in a meaningful dialogue about it? What would be your assessment of their willingness to incorporate it into the ritual expressions of the church?

4. What would your church miss if all the youth simply quit coming?

Practical Exercises for "Getting Real"

Building the Beloved Community

Gather the youth into a large room and invite them to arrange themselves in a circle. Tell them that their task is to create the type of world they want. They get to decide everything about their community, such as how they are governed, who gets to live in their world, what kinds of behavior are acceptable and unacceptable, and what the punishment is for transgression. Have them choose a record keeper who writes on a large easel or newsprint everything the community decides. Have them decide the following components:

- Government
- Religion
- Gender roles

- Marital statuses
- Vocations
- Add your own categories

This exercise is extremely intense, and adults should not worry if it gets a bit rowdy. The goal is to make sure youth are confronted with every question in society and that they determine what they find tolerable. Press questions like these: *Is premarital sex against the law here? Why? Or, can all different kinds of religions exist in your community or should there be only one? Why? Or, can a lesbian be loved in your community or will she be expelled? Why?* It is critical to press youth to answer the hard questions so they can see places where their theology could be oppressive to another. Adult youth leaders should listen attentively so they are prepared to explain how some of the positions youth espouse could be problematic. To do this exercise well, youth should be given at least an hour to engage one another before adults intervene. Discuss the implications of the choices they make about who is or is not included in the community. A follow-up session may be warranted.

Critical Cinema

Ask youth to select a popular black movie. Bring the movie and have youth watch it together. Engage in a discussion on critical issues emerging from the movie related to the following:

- Identity of the characters
- Stereotypes
- Language
- Music
- Relational dynamics
- Add your own categories

Messages in Music

Select a popular hip-hop music artist. Play a track from the tape or CD. Next, share copies of the words and have the youth listen again and interpret the meaning. Show a copy of the music video for the same song. Have the youth analyze the images along with the words. Discuss critical issues emerging from the viewing.

Meaningful Praxis: Moving Beyond Self

Paulo Freire reminds us that critical consciousness and education as the practice of freedom necessarily leads to meaningful, liberative action. Wise counsel and dialogue, as the impartation of healthy values, knowledge, and vision, must include the troubling experiences of racism, sexism, classism, homophobia, family issues, and other concerns to which we alluded earlier.[31] Mentors serve as guides who help youth to navigate the interlocking matrix of oppression endemic to American life. But, as stated earlier, the role of a mentor must move beyond seeing that youth survive. They must thrive. This suggests that youth need to be actively involved in encountering and countering the social evils in their midst. Praxis is the ongoing movement between reflection and action. It moves us beyond contemplation and dialogue into justice-directed response. What does the practice of "doing justice" look like for black youth?

What if churches not only scheduled opportunities for youth to serve homeless people, other impoverished persons, and the elderly in their communities but also enabled them to discuss factors and formulate legislation to counter the systems that contribute to poverty and maltreatment? Wouldn't it be both appropriate and growth-producing for black youth if a black church had the courage to accompany their youth to an anti-sexism rally or to a place where bold, qualified speakers teach the importance of men and women relinquishing the supposed mantel of "divine male leadership?" Of course the biblical notion of "man as the head" would be questioned—as youth wonder how sexism can ever end if men are always in charge. This is "doing justice." Or, what if the church held a mock vote to determine views and support for a constitutional amendment banning gay marriages? Can the church open a space where such debate can be healthy and meaningful and where agreements and disagreements can be voiced? Shouldn't churches be courageous enough to invite gay and lesbian supporters to speak about the importance of gay rights? Would the majority of the congregation mock and scorn the gay rights supporters, much like the Pharisees did to Jesus? Black youth must be educated and challenged to move beyond reflection into dialogue and action in ways that enable them to meet the world with all of its complexity head-on.

Questions for Reflection and Discussion

1. Identify the needs of the community/village in your church's local area. Identify critical issues within your congregation. Does your church have ministries that respond to these needs? If so, what are those ministries? If not, why not?

2. To what extent are the youth involved in these or other areas of justice ministries? Are the educational youth ministries of your church designed to provide youth with opportunities to practice their faith in their communities and the world? If so, what are those opportunities and what impact have they had on the youths' attitudes about themselves and others? If these opportunities do not exist, explore why not and what may be done to begin them.

Practical Exercises for "Getting Real"

Exercise 1

Ask the youth of your church to identify critical issues that affect them, their communities, and the world. Responses might include, for example, racial profiling, homophobia, incarceration, capital punishment, violence against women, environmental racism, and so forth. Ask the youth to discuss, create, and plan "real" practical responses to these issues. Have them present their responses to the church at-large and schedule opportunities for youth to carry out their plan with other church members.

Exercise 2

A well-known youth has been accused of committing a heinous crime. His peers are the judge and the jury. In other words, his friends decide his fate. Of course they know him and are personally invested in protecting him. The aim here is to determine the extent to which youth are committed to justice even among their own friends. The aim is also to see if black youth judge one another more harshly than they might a stranger—a historical truth that has often led blacks to accept the notion that they are inherently more criminal than other members of society.

A "Real" Vision for the Twenty-first Century

A strong, powerful, effective twenty-first–century black church must drop the inhibitions created in former years by those who feared difference. Black people today come from both wealth and poverty; conservatism and liberalism; and education and ignorance. And youth are even more diverse. Blond hair, for example, is now mainstream among a people who once laughed at it, as are hoop earrings for boys. Fewer eighteen-year-old virgins are found in our churches today than two decades ago, and the notion of a black child reared by both a biological mother and father is practically unheard of. Put simply, the demographics of the black church have changed without the theology keeping up. Antiquated perceptions of the kingdom of God serve to hinder most black children from embracing a liberative Christ because church members fail to see how their own messed-up lives can possibly be beautiful to a perfect God.

The vision for the black church now must be to stretch our belief systems and our hermeneutic in order to make sure the gospel speaks to "real" folks in the present "real" world. Black church theology must evolve out of black people's experiences instead of being limited to literal biblical textual interpretation. "Getting real" with black youth demands it. Our youth must not be expected to go along to get along. They are far too desperate for that.

PART TWO

Called to Lead, Staying the Course

CHAPTER 4

Called to Parent:
Parenting as Ministry

Elizabeth J. Walker

Train children in the right way, and when old, they will not stray.

—Proverbs 22:6

Introduction

In the book *Like Dew Your Youth*, Eugene Peterson expresses a poignant view about adolescence and family life. He says that "the moment an adolescent appears in a family . . . the home is no longer ordinary."[1] Ordinariness somehow disappears as the adolescent takes on the task of growing up into adulthood in what is best described as a uniquely vivid way.[2] And whoever is parent—whether biological, adopted, foster, step, grandparent, or other kin—is unavoidably involved in it.[3] As the prologue suggests, the invitation to Christian parents is to embrace the experience of parenting with openness to the opportunity and gift given by God to contribute to the youths' unfolding discovery of who and Whose they are, and to find in the process new or renewed awareness of our own identities.

But how are Christian parents to go about the distinctive task of parenting adolescents? What is Christian parenting? This chapter ventures an answer to this question. The thesis of this chapter is that the functions of Christian parenting have remained constant over the centuries despite the family's undergoing radical changes. The radical changes in the family came about because of modern technology, the overemphasis on individualism, and a lack of emphasis on nurturing and relational values in wider culture. Yet, despite this, the need for parents, especially Christian parents, has not changed. In particular, this chapter argues that Christian parenting is a calling and a ministry that must be embraced not simply for our youth to survive and thrive, but for the twenty-first–century human family to survive and thrive. The goal of the chapter is to present a model of Christian parenting for black people, drawing on the Christian legacy of parenting as well as current insights gained from the family therapy movement. Special attention will be given to a family-life-cycle approach to parenting.

Parenting Within the Judeo-Christian Framework

A review of biblical, historical, and sociocultural conceptualizations of the Christian family highlights the constancy of parenting functions over time. However, the structure of the family in general and the structure of the black family in particular have changed over the years. The functions of parenting that have remained constant are of pivotal importance in our exploration of parenting in this chapter. In the process of exploring these functions, at least seven key themes will be lifted up. First, parenting is an essential form of vocation and is a calling. Second, religious values support parents nurturing children and youth. Third, parents rear children to make responsible decisions. Fourth, families function as communal, multigenerational, and extended- and non-blood kin networks. Fifth, families help youth to negotiate life-cycle tasks appropriately. Sixth, some black-family parental functions remain constant despite racial discrimination. Seventh, recent cultural trends threaten the parenting process in black families.

Called to the Vocation of Parenting: An Old Testament Command

The vocation of parenting was invoked in the Hebrew Bible. God created the human family and instructed humans to be caregivers of the earth, including caring for the whole earth community—its inhabitants and its resources. An important aspect of the care of the earth included the summons or command to procreate:

> So God created humankind in his image,
>> in the image of God he created them;
>> male and female he created them.
> God blessed them, and God said to them, "Be fruitful and multiply, and fill the earth and subdue it." (Genesis 1:27-28*a*)

An implication of this passage is that reproduction is an important and particular part of what it means to be human and to participate in the ministry of parenting. "God blessed them" and made holy the vocation of parenting. In fact, the term *vocation* comes from the Latin word *vocare*, meaning "to call." Thus, in the context of procreation and parenting, vocation is God's special call to this particular way of life. For the human being, procreation stems from this call and is God's gift and invitation to participate in or join God's desire for humans to exist in the earth community in harmony with other living creatures.[4] Parenting as ministry is also not simply a blessing, but a summons from God to persons in a marital dyad.

A subsequent passage of Scripture introduces the genesis of the family in light of dyadic social relationships. God intended the human being to care for the earth and to be in generative relationships. In this passage of Scripture, God said, "It is not good that the man should be alone; I will make him a helper as his partner" (Genesis 2:18). In this story of the first family there is no command to procreate. The emphasis is on mutuality and relationship and toward intimacy and partnership between the man and the woman. Thus, while the Genesis 1 passage emphasizes procreation as gift and command, the Genesis 2 passage emphasizes mutual self-giving and partnership, or a generative relationship that forms a relational framework for parenting (Genesis 1:27-28; 2:24).

A passage in Deuteronomy highlights love of God as central to the functions of procreation and parenting, and places the identity of family in both individual and collective terms. In this view, family is seen in terms of a whole community with a collective or shared responsibility for the lives of every member, young and old. This profound sense of the social nature of family centers on the love of God, the Author of life, and on recognizing the *loveliness* of God's supreme expression of love to be shown in the lives of human beings. It also underlines the essential task of raising children who will grow in this same love of God and the expression of God's love in community (Deuteronomy 5:29–6:1-4).[5] The passage communicates the expectation that the child should be socialized to perpetuate the religious and socio-ethical values of the communal family.

A cross-reference to the foregoing understandings of family responsibility is Malachi 2:15, where God's prophet admonishes Judah for religious and cultural indiscretions in the situation of divorce and declares that God desires "God-given offspring." There is an implicit command that parents possess godly character and produce children with godly character. Further, there is a command that fathers take the responsibility for their family by remaining with them. The centrality of godliness as a goal of parenting points to parenting as ultimately a holy task. Parenting has a particular focus and purpose. As also noted in other scriptural passages, the focus and purpose is dynamically related to nurturing the young in such a way that the knowledge of God continues to each generation forever (Genesis 18:19; Psalm 20:7) Persons, families, communities, and nations that obey God's command will be God's people.

The Malachi passage confronts us with the sobering reality that there are patterns of parental relationships that threaten the purpose of parenting and the character development of children. Parents are charged to discern the patterns of relationships that threaten the family and to institute corrections. The passage gives direction regarding the responsibility of parents to make decisions in the interest of the family. In this particular instance, fathers are called to repent, to return to the family, and to resume the God-given family role that includes the family's responsibility of rearing children to trust God and to become responsible adults. Other passages highlight that rearing children includes providing basic care and nurture, teaching children the wisdom of God, and facilitating children's acceptance of the wisdom of God as the guide for their lives (Proverbs 6:20-23).

The themes of raising children in the knowledge, love, and fear of God, and making possible children's development of godly character and wisdom persist throughout the Old Testament. This activity in the life of the family has been an important aspect of the Judeo-Christian legacy. The assumption has also persisted that if parents model godliness and provide children with necessary instruction then God's promised love, strength, blessings, and peace will attend and keep them (Psalms 103:17-18; 127; 128; 147:13-14; Proverbs 4; 17:6; 20:7; 31:28). A biblical framework for parenting provides an understanding of *vocare* as God's call for parenting that focuses on the ideals of nurture, structure, instruction, guidance, and influence of children. Should we respond to this call, God promises blessings to our children and us. In our failure to respond, our children fail to discover their valued identity and purpose in God. The whole community suffers.

Parenting from a New Testament Perspective

The New Testament Gospels and Epistles continue the tradition of parenting as ministry and vocation. The first parents mentioned in the New Testament are persons who had a profound understanding of God's purpose in their ministry. Zechariah and Elizabeth were parents of John the Baptist, who was the "forerunner" of Jesus. John came to baptize persons and to prepare them to hear the gospel (Luke 1). Mary and Joseph came to terms with the vocation of parenting when an angel visited them to announce that they would become the parents of Jesus (Luke 1; Matthew 1; 2). Joseph adopted Jesus when Jesus was born. Joseph's and Zechariah's families were related by blood. Jesus and John the Baptist each grew in the knowledge and wisdom of God and went on to fulfill their various vocations in regard to God's plan for their lives within the community of faith. The Gospel stories point to a strong tradition of parenting that provided young people with the values they inherited from family and ultimately from God.

One of the first acts of John the Baptist's and Jesus' ministries was to bring together a family of believers. They each mentored disciples in order to evoke a specific response. The mentoring process entailed educating the disciples in an ever-increasing knowledge of God. This mentoring is reminiscent of the parental task of socializing persons to appropriate and pass on important values to future generations. John the Baptist preached repentance and baptism. Jesus Christ proclaimed the gospel. Each understood himself and his social, cultural identity, and location in the context of a communal, extended, multigenerational family and religion. From the beginning, God's people were reminded of the inclusive nature of the extended family of God.

By way of summary, the Judeo-Christian heritage and tradition placed high value on the function of the family. The family was a large, multigenerational group of blood-relatives, "built around a core group known as a lineage."[6] Extended families lived together and, in most cases, traced their lineage through the descent line of the father. Families appealed to the patriarchal system in which the welfare, spiritual, and developmental needs of all family members were ideally considered and provided for. The patriarchal family system insisted on the integrity and well-defined social roles of each member of the family and extended family/community members. Attention was given to mutual concern for children by extended family members. Rearing children extended beyond the boundaries of kinship into the wider community in accordance with rules and limits that balanced and assured appropriate relationships. Within the religious and socio-ethical context of the extended community system, as well as within the family, children were recipients of love, care, and nurture. Integrity, security, stability, valued identity, protection, individual roles, and tradition were important core values of the Judeo-Christian family system.

The Legacy of African American Parenting

The view of the family expounded in the Judeo-Christian tradition influenced the black family. Black families tended to be large, multigenerational, extended, blood and non-blood kin, who, in most cases, traced their lineage through the male parent. The unique situation of slavery, racism, and the influence of acculturation in the American context created a unique challenge to black people. Out of this challenge came resilience and adaptive strategies that have proved to be critical for the preservation of black family core values. For black people, family referred to extended family members living within and beyond a given household.[7]

Despite the instance of slavery and the system of separating black families, research indicates that the incidence of "female-headed households did not change much in 200 years."[8] More than three-fourths of black households were headed by male and female. After slavery ended, black people who were able to acquire land tended to "re-create kin networks that resembled African extended families and compounds."[9] Social networks provided essential support for survival and adaptation in the American context.[10] Like their African ancestors, black families placed a high value on child bearing and child rearing, supported by the care, nurture, and training of children. Socialization of children almost always involved thoughtful strategies to protect the children from the harshness of racism for as long as possible, while preparing children to conceptualize the family as the "mediating link between the individuals' self-concept and the racial group."[11] Black families socialized teens to appropriate and safeguard the family-values system and maintain a healthy sense of self and ethnic identity in a hostile racial environment.

Andrew Billingsley's analyses of ancient African data support in part the argument that the strength of black families over time has been rooted in a distinctive set of patterns brought by the slaves from Africa.[12] His research uncovered "ethical codes" that centered on the value of a communal multigenerational environment of both blood and non-blood kin supported by a communal spirituality. Billingsley asserts that these "ethical codes" continued in black family systems in America. Despite the devastation of slavery, many slaves and their descendents were able to transmit the essential core communal value to new generations.

Over time, many black Americans have been acculturated to the dominant cultural theme that places high value on the individualization of self and on the nuclear family. However, Billingsley found that, especially among black Americans with low incomes and those with low levels of acculturation of dominant values, the African multigenerational and extended family values prevailed. These core values have been less prevalent among black Americans who have a high level of acculturation in American culture.[13]

An important point here is that the African communal spirituality and the survival of this spirituality in black family life in America connects with the Judeo-Christian legacy found in Scripture. And, during the era of slavery and afterward, communal responsibility for raising and nurturing children was a core value that was transmitted to new generations. Indeed, the ability of black families and black children to continue on amidst the unique realities of life faced by them depended on their embracing and living this value.

The Black Family of the Twenty-first Century

The structure of the black family has undergone tremendous change, particularly over the final thirty years of the twentieth century. The enormity of this change is found in the circumstances of family life and the changing configuration of families who are responsible for the welfare of children. Research indicates that there has been a decline in marriage but not in the desire for long-term romantic relationships among black American adults.[14] Moreover, there is an emerging trend of declining proportions of black children living with both parents, and increasing numbers living with their mothers in single-parent households, with grandparent and other kin caregivers, and in foster care. Foster care has risen in the last decade, with black children representing "a disproportionate number who live in institutions, group homes, and with foster families."[15] The incidence of poverty among this population placed increasing numbers of children at risk for chronic poverty and placement in non-traditional living arrangements.[16] Research also indicates black family resiliency in the face of tremendous racial and economic challenges in some ways has been supported by social programs sponsored by the religious congregations. Some social programs alleviate the stress imposed upon black families due to stratification of the labor market and racial discrimination.

A definition of the modern African American family is not limited to a study of social problems, demographics, or structure. Rather, a complete understanding of black families involves exploring means by which families impart specific strategies to its members to ensure its resiliency and adaptation.[17] The black religious community has long been an organizing and supportive institution that provides religious and social support to the family. For example, "many black churches promote formal and informal mechanisms of family support."[18] Congregations emphasize the importance of multigenerational families as a locus for the transmission of family values and the support of the larger family system to include the congregation. Historically, the quality of life for black people has been enhanced through the maintenances of relationships with religious institutions.

The important point to be made here is that there is a history of the parenting function that must remain a focal point in these families in the twenty-first century. The value of parenting as ministry to which God calls and blesses us is pivotal and evokes the authority for Christian parents to establish and perpetuate the reign of God. As part of this orientation, parenting is seen as a spiritual value. Christian parenting functions to support parents' nurture of youth to become God-given and godly offspring who are not only knowledgeable about their value imbued by God but also about how to live in light of their social, cultural, and ultimate reality. Youth are nurtured and equipped so that they may make responsible decisions about their relationships with self, God, and others at the appropriate life-cycle transition (1 Corinthians 13:11; Proverbs 20:11).

The black family has typically functioned as a communal, multigenerational, extended family of blood and non-blood kin that fostered the integrity, spiritual growth, and development of all family members. The continuation of this framework is vital to the nurture of our youth. In addition, the role of the extended family, church, and community in rearing our youth to eventually assume adult roles at the appropriate life-cycle stage of development must persist. Congregational life has been an important support for the multigenerational family as a locus for transmitting values across generations. The point of this review is that the black family has been and must continue to be resilient in the face of racial discrimination and marginalizing practices in the American social milieu, economy, and politics. This means keeping focus on the parenting function despite recent trends in the structure of the black family that can place present and future generations of youth at an increasing risk for problematic development and diminished hope.

The many changes black families have experienced in recent years provide a real danger that must not be overlooked. We must not take our attention off the many youth who are in situations away from relatives who could impart a sense of self-value and inculcate in them a positive and enlivening understanding of their cultural heritage, and personal and ethnic identity. Far too many of our youth are in prison and have lost the opportunity for the direct socializing influences of community and family. Yet they must not be forgotten. Some researchers refer to our "lost" youth as having a truncated life cycle, not having the time in the family and community to prepare for adult roles and responsibilities appropriately.[19] Some of our parents, too, are largely acculturated and operate from an individualistic rather than a communal paradigm of family.

Regardless of the structure of the family and the current situation, the task of parenting has not changed much from generation to generation. Parenting requires spirituality, vision, purpose, flexibility, and a frame. Christian parenting is the theological imperative—the *vocatio*, or voice of God calling—for the human family and the modern family to stay the course. This is, in fact, the call to black parents for the continuation of a real vocation on behalf of present and future generations of youth.

Toward a Model of Christian Parenting

The Christian parent is called by God to embrace the following characteristics: to place Jesus Christ at the center of value and meaning; to be emotionally differentiated or be able to separate what one feels from the feelings of others, while being emotionally connected to others; to be socially interdependent with others and not isolated; and to appeal to a set of core values that add texture and assistance to the function of parenting. Christian parents interpret their parenting experiences in the light of the saving activity of God. Further, the Christian parent responds to the three generational life-cycle demands for development and growth of all family members, thus fulfilling developmental tasks that prepare family members to participate in society. All of these characteristics are built into a theoretical model that describes the parental role and how it promotes developmental growth.

The specific dimensions of a parenting model help to foster a parenting environment that provides the following:

1. Flexibility that fosters interdependence between the teen and other members of the family;

2. A sense of comfort where parents are at-home with their sexual selves in ways that assist teens to be comfortable with their own sexuality;

3. A sense of comfort with parents' spiritual selves in ways that facilitate teen spirituality;

4. Decision-making opportunities for the teen within the family system; and

5. Boundaries that provide sufficient structure, along with support, for youth to accomplish specific age-related developmental tasks.

Above all, parents must maintain a caring, supportive family structure that propels teens toward autonomy, while not coercing them prematurely into the world. Earlier I made reference to the life cycle of some black teens being disrupted, and age-specific developmental tasks curtailed. This often occurs when black teens are either forced out of the home prematurely or forced into adult roles and life events without appropriate mentoring.

Christian parenting enables the developmental growth of youth by drawing on a life-cycle approach to family development. A life-cycle approach to parenting begins with young adults who have developed a good enough sense of differentiated self-identity, and are ready to join with another person of the opposite sex in order to form a marital relationship and to raise children.

A life-cycle approach for parenting youth involves the family life cycle, which has four stages: formation, expansion, contraction, and post-parental stages.[20] Moreover, there are several different life cycles within the family life cycle, including individual and marital. Particular focus here is on the expansion stage where parents must provide the kind of family growth environment for the individual life cycles of the youth to flourish.

Ideally, the family life cycle begins with the formation stage. Here the couple meets, engages practices of courting and getting to know each other, and finally marries. Following the marriage, they decide to have children, and the marital dyad expands. This is called the expansion stage of the family.

The expansion stage of the family life cycle involves parental tasks that include the responsibility to (1) accommodate new family members; (2) provide for physical and economic needs of family members; (3) establish, maintain, and balance appropriate interactions as well as emotional and developmental needs of the family members; (4) provide socialization of family members within and outside the family; and (5) appropriately affiliate with multigenerational and extended family kin and family networks.[21] During the contraction stage, children become young adults and are launched into the world. When all the children are launched, the family is in the post-parental stage.

Parenting teens calls for other tasks as well. For example, families have ideal child and teen images. These images are the expectations that parents have of their children from the time they are conceived until the children are launched. The task for the parents is to revise these ideal teen images in light of the actual or real teen in their family.[22] Parents must also help youth to set appropriate behavioral boundaries so that youth make the right decisions within and outside the home. Parents also need to make sure they do not abdicate from the parental role, and only turn decision making over to teens when they demonstrate age-appropriate skills. Premature decision-making will overwhelm the youth and create many emotional problems. Thus parents need to know what age-appropriate decisions teens should be making. Parents need to be sure that teens establish relationships within their own age cohort as well as to have appropriate age-related relationships across generations. For example, teens need relationships with grandparents and aunts and uncles, as well as with younger children whom they can guide and nurture. Teens also need encouragement to do tasks related to testing their growth and identity in the world so that they discover their gifts that need developing for the future. The teen years afford parents the opportunity to release family members to the extended and larger community appropriately.

Not only do parents have life-cycle related tasks, youth have individual life cycle tasks, the main one consisting of learning to be a relatively independent adult vocationally, educationally, and socially.[23] The developmental tasks of teens include:

- Differentiating sufficiently from the family of origin to becoming relatively an autonomous self, while maintaining appropriate relationships with one's family of origin;

- Making appropriate progress toward independent young adulthood, moving toward establishing of self vocationally and economically;
- Establishing appropriate and satisfactory sexual outlets;
- Establishing appropriate and adequate social and personal relationships; and
- Beginning to demonstrate the ability to function interdependently and in a socially responsible manner, while maintaining a firm sense of personal and social identity.

The contraction stage of family life in which young adults are launched involves several relational tasks for the parents. These tasks include:

- Releasing teen family members appropriately;
- Providing for physical and economic needs of teens;
- Adjusting limits and boundaries to afford teens increased responsibility for decisions and consequences;
- Balancing adolescence needs for freedom and independence with appropriate assumption of responsibility;
- Adjusting the parents' corresponding relinquishment of total responsibility for launched young adults, with the continuing need for communication to deal with changing relations between generations;
- Providing for socialization of teens into mature roles within the family, and socialization for their later adult life of making choices related to vocation and marriage; and
- Providing teens with appropriate affiliation opportunities with the extended family and kinship network and friendship networks.

The parental system supports the growth and development of each family member. The relationship task of the parents supports and accommodates the needs of the evolving teen for increased autonomy without sacrificing the ongoing needs for parental limits.

Staying the Course in Real Parenting

A three-generational orientation to parenting tasks is particularly relevant in parenting teens because these tasks serve as preparation for teens to accept adult responsibilities and commitments. This orientation includes the children, parents, and grandparents. The three-generational view calls upon parents to reorganize limits/boundaries to permit opportunities for teen autonomy and independence. This view of family transformation accounts for the shifts in relationships across generations that occur during the launching of a teen. When teens demand more autonomy and independence in the family, the following must be attended to:

- Parents and grandparents redefine their relationships. Unresolved problems between parents and grandparents resurface.
- Spouses renegotiate their marital contract and their marital, family, and personal convictions and beliefs about themselves and teens.
- Parents with low levels of self-differentiation from their families of origin often fear the loss of the teen. This is particularly the case when the teen has been used to substitute for an unavailable parent. The teen's role, assignment, and importance to the functioning of the family may create a source of anxiety when the teen attempts to differentiate from the family. Triangles or family attempts to draw teens into marital or family conflict and to take sides across generations may surface. When this happens, it often leads to disrupting the life-cycle tasks of the young adult.

There are individual life-cycle tasks and demands on each parent that affect the life-cycle tasks of teens and young adults. For example, while working on their own midlife issues, parents facilitate the teens' maturation into young adulthood in two critical areas: the establishment of a solid self-identity, and actively mentoring the teen in the development of a sense of a valued ethnic self that is uniquely given by God as gift. The task is to help the youth answer positively the question "Who am I?" Sometimes the individual life-cycle demands on the parents make it difficult for them to allow youths to individuate and leave home. Where this happens, the launching of the young adult is prolonged.

Finally, launching teens into young adulthood involves transmitting values that will sustain them through the young adult period and further. These values must have been evident through-out the rearing of the child, and necessarily reflect the faith values of the parents. The social norms and values of the Judeo-Christian faith, the African heritage, and black American legacy provide rich resources for creating a fund of wisdom that can shape the mentoring-and-launching process of youth into young adulthood. The values inform gender identification, social and cultural values, and socialization in male/female roles and relationships. In addition, traditional communal values found in black congregations also provide important resources of use in the launching process. Values taught in churches and in homes by black people support the solidification of identity and draw attention to social and political concerns that ultimately affect the family.

Some Concluding Comments

The dominant concept of family expounded on in this chapter is multigenerational and communal and embraces an extended-family orientation of blood and non-blood kin. A rich foundation for the understanding of the Christian family and parenting is the concept of vocation that centers on God's call for parenting to be ministry in the human family of God. Parents with a solid sense of self-identity, self in community, and self-responsibility tend to experience success in communicating and exhibiting Christian values and appropriate boundaries and limits to their children within the context of extended family and community relationships. The children of parents with firm, clear boundaries and limits are most successful in negotiating the transition of persons from adolescence to young adulthood. Spiritual values provide the framework for preparing teens to take on adult roles. The Bible clearly instructs parents to love, to respect, and to teach a way of being in relationships and the world that emulates God's love and *loveliness*. Christian parents must be grounded in a faith community and tradition, be willing to conceptualize family as the primary Christian educational context, develop a sense of personal and communal spirituality, and must be prepared to pass the tradition to the next generation.

The Judeo-Christian faith tradition has resources to assist parents in clarifying modern-day issues that occur in parenting ministry. It is the responsibility of the Christian community today to clarify our values to our teens, drawing on biblically based ethical guidelines to help teens journey toward positive or valued self-identity. Parenting our adolescents is real ministry that holds both challenge and promise. It is an essential ministry that must be undertaken for the sake of today's and tomorrow's youth.

Questions for Reflection and Discussion

1. What does parenting as ministry mean to you? Of what importance is making one's Christian faith apparent in the task of parenting?

2. What challenges do you or families in your church and community face that call for measures of care, support, and guidance of the parents? The children?

3. How do you or the parents in your church and community balance the needs of self and the parenting tasks?

4. What opportunities are there for parents to share and support one another? What would you like to see your church do to help you or other parents carry out the vocation of parenting? With whom will you share your ideas?

CHAPTER 5

Hope in the Midst of Struggle: Church and Parents Together in Raising Teens

Tapiwa Mucherera

The youth may walk faster than the elder, but it is the elder who knows the way.

What an elder can see sitting, a child cannot see while standing.

—Zimbabwean proverbs

Introduction: The Village, Ours to Keep

When I think of the term "village" from the standpoint of my home country of Zimbabwe, Africa, my thoughts turn to the understanding that hope can never fail those united in their struggle. In the African tradition, "it is not *my* village; it is *our* village to keep." Everyone has a share of responsibility about what goes on in the village. We talk of "our" children, not just "my" children. As adults we have an unspoken agreement giving one another permission to raise "our kids," and the children understand this informal agreement. If I see someone's child misbehaving and I ignore it, that child is going to influence my child's behavior to do the same thing. In correcting the misbehaving child, I am being proactive in nipping the problem before it spreads to other children. Children who grow in an environment where they are given respect and are provided with a sense of community will give respect to the adults of the community.

There should be no child left an orphan as long as there are adults in the community. A Shona[1] saying, *Nherera teeerera panorangwa vana wevamwe*, translates to "The orphan pays attention when in the midst of other parents giving wise counsel to their children." Any adult is aware that when he or she gives counsel to his/her children in the midst of orphans, the counsel he or she gives is for the good of the orphans as well. In that moment, the adult treats the orphan as his or her own. The orphans, or those who feel orphaned (abandoned by parents emotionally, physically, and so forth), have hope in the adults in the wider community of wisdom. The adults don't have to be blood parents; anyone the children consider to be "good enough" can be informally an adopted parent.

In the village that we regard as "our" village, people hold each other accountable. Members know that what affects one exerts an effect on everybody, and the effect it exerts on a neighbor affects oneself. There is an unspoken understanding in the village that we were created for relationships, interdependence, and were never created as islands. Communal cooperation is valued rather than competition with the "Joneses." The village provides the welcoming and guiding environment needed for the child's sense of belonging and maturation physically, psychologically, and spiritually. Communal rituals incorporate and affirm the child's place and participation in community life. Involving the child in community life that discloses cultural and religious values seeks to influence the child's affirmation of who and Whose he/she is and his/her identity formation.

The colonial and imperialist attitudes about a village as backward, which were communicated to Zimbabweans during the era of colonization, were based on a materialistic and capitalistic culture that defined, for example, the mud houses and grass thatched huts as a sign of backwardness and primitivism. The cultural values of the people were judged by what the people possessed, not by their communal, religious, and relational values. But a village is more than a compound of huts or houses. What makes a village are the people who are "the living" and the "living dead," or the "cloud of witnesses" composed of deceased loved ones whose memories and spirit remain alive in community. Village also includes the environment (nature, animals, rivers, and so forth); communal mores and ethics; the stories told of the past and present; and a sense of belonging spiritually, psychologically, and physically to the community. A village is because of the persons who live in it, and a person is because of others.

Munhu vanhu is a Shona saying that translates to "a person is because of other people." This saying illuminates the way Shona people define the self. Other common African sayings support the idea that the worldview, philosophy, and self-understanding of most Africans is community-based. One of the sayings already appears in preceding chapters: "I am because we are; and since we are, therefore I am." Others include "One tree does not make a forest"; and "A charcoal or coal gets its burning energy from being in the fire of others." Out of interpersonal relations one develops an individual identity. Humans get their vitality, their physical, social, psychological, and spiritual security, and their identity from being in healthy interpersonal relationships with others.[2]

I share these thoughts about the village because, in my work with black families in the United States, I am reminded of an essential need to bring new or renewed awareness to the functions of the village in our current day-to-day living in the United States. This need has already been echoed in the preceding chapters of this book. However, in this chapter we will explore in more detail the kinds of tensions or struggles arising, especially between parental figures and teens, in the lives of black people here in this Western context. The chapter will also explore guides for addressing tensions within the family setting, and it will suggest roles for the church as "village" to play in helping parental figures think through what is needed to rear teens and be "good enough" guides. These roles will be presented from the standpoint of a re-villaging model or a way of reclaiming vital village values and functions. My intent is to make clear that re-villaging efforts are essential, if the congregation is to be the "village of hope" to which the prologue refers. In the basis of this assertion, the final section will challenge the church to be the village of hope.

The Struggle: Rearing Teens in Today's Black Village Life

Today's black families go about their everyday lives under remarkably varied circumstances. Many function admirably well,

85

including those in dire situations of inadequate support and guidance where much is required of both teens and parents.[3] However, capitalism and individualism are shaking the sense of community and the foundations of black family values. Some of the core values, such as a sense of community, are being eroded and are threatening black people's sense of communal identity. Many communities comprise people who live next door to each other without really knowing one another. Due to mobility, blood relatives no longer necessarily live next door or even in the same state. There is a loss of the extended family support. The buffer to societal problems faced by those who parent the youth is steadily disappearing.[4]

The reality is that black communities are witnessing dysfunctional families; struggling poor families; single-parent families; gang activities; drugs and alcohol; disproportionate incidences of incarceration; children's desensitization to violence as they watch more and more of it on television and in real life; and the sexualization of electronic media through portrayal of pornographic images.[5] Moreover, an estimated 50 percent of children in foster care are black.[6] These problems, bundled together with identity confusion caused by ever-changing American cultural values, have left youth with no "home" physically, culturally, or religiously.

Chapter 3 has already reminded us of the dire need of mentors and adults to invest self, time, and resources for the sake of black youths' hope-filled sojourn in life. This need is particularly critical with children in homes where the father is not present. A study reported by Boyd-Franklin from the Center for the Study of Social Policy and Philadelphia's Children's Network estimates that 50 percent of black children grow up without fathers who are present in the household. The consequences have been significant, especially in the case of young black males who need male guidance for their transition to manhood.[7] But Nichols and Good confirm that an added issue is that "today's families tend to be more heterogeneous and busier with more and varied tasks. Divorce is common, and although it saves many youth from abusive households[,] others are also harmed when messy divorces inappropriately involve them . . . Families are busy, and members are consumed with their own activities."[8]

Media have played an enormous role in shaping youths' sexual norms and pressing beyond previous boundaries of sexual behavior. It is difficult to get clear measurements of youths' sexual practices. However, there are data showing that black youth, along with Latino youth, are having sex at earlier ages and that across all racial ethnic groups there appear to be increasing numbers—especially younger youth—who engage in oral sex, thinking that it "is not as big a deal as intercourse."[9] Too many teens are uninformed about the risks of oral sex, since they mistakenly regard it as safe sex. And they are inadequately informed and protected from the consequences of sexual activity.[10] It is important, however, to add the good news that teenage pregnancy among all racial ethnic groups continues to decline. Also, the rate of abortions has decreased even though, proportionately, more pregnancies end in abortion among adolescents than among women over age twenty.[11] The role of parents or guardians is a formidable one. Yet there is evidence that youth and parents both need and want information about sex.[12]

What can bring hope in the situation black village families find themselves today? I propose that "good enough" courageous parents with the support and action of a caring church are our hope. The role of the church is a pivotal one. Specifically, our hope is in efforts of the church and the whole community to "catch" the vision of re-villaging.

Hope in the Village: A Few "Good Enough" Courageous Parents and a Caring Church

Re-villaging, as stated earlier, is the idea of reclaiming the core values of traditional Africa that gave people a sense of communal identity. The definition of *re-villaging* used in this chapter is borrowed from an unpublished paper presented by Drs. Edward Wimberly and Tapiwa Mucherera in Cameroon, West Africa. Our position in that paper was that re-villaging is an essential attempt to reestablish selective village functions such as symbolizing, supporting/maintaining, ritualizing, and mentoring. The symbolizing function regards the organizing of village life around a particular story and sub-stories that form an overarching system capable of giving meaning to every aspect of life. The support/maintenance function provides cross-generational relational ties for people that help them maintain emotional, physical, and spiritual well-being in the face of life transitions and difficulty. The mentoring function entails providing opportunities for the next generation to be integrated into the community's meaning system in ways that result in their internalization of helpful and growth-producing attitudes, scenes, roles, and story plots. The ritualizing function provides repetitive patterns for reinforcing symbolizing, support/maintenance, and mentoring functions.[13]

There is great hope in our present village. Jesus did not choose one hundred disciples, but twelve (actually eleven) who were committed to changing the world. When they started they were even hiding because they were afraid of being killed by the same people to whom they were trying to bring good news. When churches and communities declare they are going to take back their streets, they are declaring war against drug dealers and prostitutes whose targets are the same youth the churches are trying to protect. Drug dealers will kill parents or other adults for trying to keep the community teenagers from being corrupted. Boyd-Franklin asserts that "the organized church is by far the most profound instrument available to Blacks when it comes to coping with the multiplicity of problems that beset their lives. Church members as well as nonmembers accept . . . the church and use the church to confront their own helpless and depressive attitudes and oppressive practices toward them by others."[14]

Re-villaging is quite a venture. It is a critical part of our attempt to "keep it real" in our work with black youth. Below are a few actions that parents and the church take in the process of rearing black youth.

Parents, Live an Exemplary Life

If there is going to be any "real-ness" in the re-villaging process, it has to start within the homes in which youth are raised. The character of our children is largely influenced by the values, behaviors, principles, and morals of parental figures. It is important that the parent strives to be a role model to his or her own children. For example, parents who come home drunk or use drugs, thinking the children won't find out, lie to themselves. Mothers and fathers who are unfaithful to each other, and single parents whose relationships and sexual activities in and beyond the home belie meanings of commitment, send negative messages to their children about standards of behavior. These instances send a particularly acute message with respect to Christian parenting. When parents lead a life that is contradictory to what we profess is right in the Christian walk, the youth ask: "Don't the adults know that we see the contradiction between the Christian lifestyle they preach to us and the lives they actually model before us?" The message is clear! In other words, we as parents are called to practice what we preach; and we are to do so before our children consistently. Jay Kesler says:

> If children see no difference between the way their believing parents handle problems and the way the unbelieving parents of their friends handle similar situations, they will probably question their parents' faith and with good reason. . . .
>
> [I]f parents refuse to acknowledge their wrong-doing and try to deceive their children by lying, misleading, or covering up the sin, usually the child begins a spiritual decline. Resentment often sets in, and the disillusioned child begins a long journey through a spiritual desert.[15]

As Christian parents we are to live by the morals that we want our children to follow. The basic foundations for the Christian life are built in the home. Of course the church's role is to help parents strengthen the values youth need, but we must live those values by example in what we say and do within and outside the home. Our spirituality as Christians matters! It is also important for parents to talk openly with teens about the role of spirituality in the journey of life—its importance and why. Establish family rituals, including prayers at meal and at other times, and occasions for sharing concerns, fears, thoughts and questions about God. Youth want to talk, and as parents we need to share our spiritual beliefs and stories of how we have overcome adversity or worked through tough decisions as the result of our faith.[16] Praying for our children is also a pivotal part of how we express our spirituality as Christians.

Set Boundaries and Accountability, But Don't Overdo It

It is important for parents to know where their teens are and with whom. Set curfew and clear limits or boundaries, and stick to them. We may tell our children to call if they are going to be late, and to let us know where they are and when they expect to be home. If we give our child a curfew and we are asleep every time he/she gets home, and we do not bother to inquire about the reasons for his/her failure to get home on time, it shows the curfew to be just a gimmick. There is no accountability.

There is no child who does not want boundaries, even though he/she presses to bend or expand the boundaries. The developmental stage of adolescence entails the task of acquiring skills necessary for gaining autonomy and making personal decisions. It also entails being accountable for those decisions. This is a gradual process and does not mean that all the bonds of parental love, care, guidance, and responsibility cease. All of these qualities of parenthood are necessary parts of assisting the adolescent's gradual movement toward maturity. Chapter 2 emphasized the importance of attentiveness during what is often called the "rebellious period" of life. It is important to reemphasize here that "real" care of our youth is being attentive to the difficulty they have in balancing their need for independence with dependence.

Undertaking the task is not easy. Harley Atkinson reminds us that carrying it out "is often an origin of conflict between adolescents and their parents, and a source of stress for both."[17] And the greater stress may be experienced by parents—a situation that sometimes requires help and guidance for struggling parents. In this regard, "real" village ministry with youth necessarily expands to "keeping it real" with parents through providing opportunities such as parents' forums in which they share their stories, receive mutual support, and explore parenting skills. In the face of tough decisions, parents groups or forums such as those given by the Youth Hope-Builders Academy of Interdenominational Theological Center provide a time and space for "talk time," role-playing, and gaining wisdom from a skillful guide and other parents.

We must also be aware that our youth will not be exactly like us, nor should we expect them to be. Therefore our task is to try not to mold them into our own image. In addition, each teen is different and should never be compared to siblings or teenage relatives. Our parental role is to affirm the unique qualities and strengths of the youth as means of helping them grow to be their own person and maintain a positive belief in the self. A helpful approach in parents' forums is to invite parents to:

- identify the qualities and strengths of their teens;
- describe when and how the parents became aware of the qualities and strengths; and
- explore ways of affirming and encouraging further development of the teen's qualities and strengths.

Forge Real Relationships and Communication

One of the basic values for a "good enough" parent is having real relationships and open communication with our children. What our youth want from us in a good relationship is more than money. Research on youth who have been involved in catastrophic school shootings came from wealthy families where they experienced parental deprivation, little nurturance, and/or physical, sexual, and emotional abuse.[18] Atkinson cites the results of a study undertaken by Gordon Sebine in which "79 percent of the parents involved reported that they were communicating well with their teenagers. On the other hand, in a complete reversal, 81 percent of the teenagers said that their parents were not communicating with them."[19] Atkinson goes on to say: "This study indicates first, that there is little common understanding between parents and teenagers as to what good communication is, and second, that a large percentage of adolescents recognize the need for better communication in the home."[20]

Youth need real communication with parents that allows them to talk about their issues, interests, and problems; and youth are bothered by insufficiency, ineffectiveness, or lack of communication.[21] The research of McWhirter and his associates also affirms that good interpersonal relationships between parents and children help counter many of the problems that our youth face, including those related to sex or other risky behaviors.[22] Consequently, one of the goals of "keeping it real" in youth ministry in the re-villaging model must necessarily give attention to strategies that contribute to the formation of effective communication between parents and teens. For example, parents' forums may focus on:

- teaching communication skills such as inviting conversation;
- attentiveness; listening; uses and meanings of non-verbal communication; the role and uses of questioning, tending to conflict, and follow-up; and

- providing intergenerational activities that not simply bring parents and teens together but also engage them in discussion and role-plays on relevant issues.

Teach About Sexuality

What kind of a parent would start applauding if a naked man or woman would walk into their home? But isn't that what we are doing when we order cable TV and Internet for our children without supervision and restrictions or censorship concerning what our children are allowed to watch. The fastest growing industry on the Internet is said to be the pornographic industry. Just as in other addictions such as tobacco, the pornographic industry believes in "catching them early and keeping them for life." When our teens are addicted, it is hard for them to break the habit even as adults. Today, "pairing of" and dating is happening at earlier ages, often in middle school; and our youth also gather in a wide range of social settings where adult supervision is lacking and sexual exploration occurs. McWhirter and his associates also claim that many black youth today perceive sexual activity as a rite of passage from adolescence into adulthood. Many teens believe that the way to develop an adult identity is by engaging in sexual intercourse. In addition, some teens use sexual activity as a way to attain independence and individuality.[23] Yet, unfortunately, their sexual activity often results in premature parenthood.

We need to teach our youth that having sex does not equal being a real man or woman. In addition, sex is not synonymous with love but is an emotion. The media has confused our children by insinuating that having sex equals "making love." True love is not made through sexual intercourse. Self-respect, respect for others, and being responsible is more honorable than bragging about with how many women one has had sexual intercourse. However, in order for this kind of parental guidance to occur, many parents will need to overcome their embarrassment in talking with teens about sex. We as parents need to be proactive in our relational connection with youth in deference to complaining about media messages that go against our values, or about our teens' discovery of answers to their curiosity and questions on their own.

At the same time, we as parents must not be naïve in thinking that our youth do not already know about sexual matters. They do! And they have gleaned information and ideas from school, the media, magazines, and peers. However, what they need from us is the right application of the information. Most parents won't comment on bad sexualized commercials or TV shows when something inappropriate comes on. This is the time for parents to engage in conversations with teens about what is wrong or right about the sexualized scenes. In this regard, the kind of real communication discussed in the preceding section is essential. In the re-villaging model, churches "keep it real" in activities that reduce the reticence of parents to engage in real communication, including the following:

- Introduce parents to materials that provide handles on approaching the topic of sex with teens. One example is *The Big Talk Book: Parents, Teens, and Sex,* by Bruce Cook.[24]
- Invite parents into a discussion on the values they hold on sexual relationships, sources and reasons for these values, and ways of discussing their values with teens.
- Engage parents in role-plays of parent-teen conversations on sex.

Teach Ways to Defend Against Violence and Racism

Violence and racism are imbedded in the American culture. As black parents, we cannot blind our eyes to these realities and appear shocked when youth experience and react to them. Kesler says, "Bad influences are everywhere, and there is no way to keep kids away from them. The choice we do have is how we will influence the way our kids interpret this negative input."[25]

With regard to violence, gangs on TV send messages to our youth that the "one who dies with the most toys wins." Rather, the message should be "the one who dies with the most toys dies." Some of the games youth play and movies they watch are very violent. Violence and rape in dating relationships happen. Parental involvement means monitoring our teens, keeping avenues to "real" communication open. Especially regarding sexual abuse that happens not simply in dating but in families, the re-villaging model includes teaching youth and apprising parents about what is and is not appropriate sexual behavior. This includes emphasizing the privacy of the body, the right not to be touched in any place that one does not want to be touched, and the right as an individual to say that a particular kind of touch is unwanted. It also includes apprising parents that sexual abuse and incest have disastrous long-term consequences for youth, and that these acts constitute criminal behavior and are punishable by law.[26]

Racial violence is a reality in the American context. Racism still exists, and our teens need to know that this is not a made-up problem. As parents, we need to teach our children ways to defend themselves without being violent, and ways of responding to police and other authorities in cases of racial profiling. The re-villaging model assists this action by involving parents and youth together in the following:

- Invite youths' stories of their experiences of racism;
- Explore the effect experiences of racism have had on them;
- Engage in role-plays of experiences of racism that are followed by exploring ways of handling them (for example, role-play an incident of racial profiling by police in which you keep hands free and clearly visible, and exhibit polite and accommodating behavior; or dramatize the following: "You are personally insulted verbally by a racist remark or implication. How do you handle it?"[27]).

Single Parents, Don't Go It Alone

Boyd-Franklin and Franklin suggest that single parents not doubt their ability based on previous generations; find support from a single-parent support group or extended family; find some role models from the community or the extended family for their children; not go it alone or isolate themselves, but to find help in co-parenting the children, using grandparents if available; and talk to others to get encouragement and support.[28] The main thing for single parents is to stay connected and have a network of friends and relatives to help when needed. Boyd-Franklin and Franklin further say that many single mothers have sought for their sons other male role models among their extended families and communities. With the help of these willing men, many single mothers have been able to provide strength, structure, love, guidance, and strong family bonds for their sons, in spite of the odds.[29]

Even though there are studies indicating that children raised in fatherless homes suffer emotionally, other studies indicate that "this, in part, may be corrected by the black child's opportunity to have male models among the male kinsmen in his extended family network."[30] It is essential for single parents to seek other trusted members in the community to watch out for their teens, giving such people permission to correct the teens when they are in the wrong. The parent is to let the child know that there are several adults in the community watching and that these adults have permission to correct the child when the child is doing something wrong.

Church, Be the Village of Hope

Boyd-Franklin says that the church is the main social support system for most black families, after the extended family. Consequently, one often hears black people refer to the church as their "church home." This is because the church not only offers spiritual support but also serves in providing relationships, fellowship, advice, and social activities for the whole family. Churches "function as surrogate families for isolated and overburdened single mothers."[31] Surrogate parental help becomes real through the support, leadership, and care given within the church by both laymen and laywomen and by men and women beyond the church walls. Men mentoring young men is pivotal, and women helping single parents outside of church activities reflects an important sense of solidarity. When the church functions in this way, it actualizes the meaning of the "village." The following suggestions are also ways for the village to be of service to parents and their teens.

Believe in Our Teens

The church today appears to be the church for adults only. Churches have to evaluate themselves to see if they are welcoming to teenagers. As chapters 2 and 3 have stated, once teenagers feel unwelcome and treated as invisible they won't come back. Churches have to treat their teens as "the church of today and tomorrow." Many of our teenagers know how to run computers better than many adults. Churches can easily ask the youth of the church to take turns adding art to the Sunday bulletin, with adult supervision. Sunday bulletin covers for September through May could be easily created during the summer while the teens are on vacation from school. When we allow our youth to take leadership as liturgists, form their own choir, and involve their input in major decisions as a church, we grow them into leaders. Man Kueng Ho supports this point with his statement that "[t]he churches were, and often still are, one of the few places where black men and women could feel that they were respected for their own talents and abilities. The community church also became one of the most important sources of leadership experience and development in the black community."[32]

The importance of engaging our teens in church activities cannot be overemphasized. Once teenagers realize the importance of church and are given a place in church, they are less likely to leave. Boyd-Franklin says: "Studies have shown that young men who had gone to church as children were less likely to become involved in gangs, drugs, and crime as adults. It is very important that we continue to encourage our sons to attend church with us as a family, even when Sunday morning church attendance begins to compete with Saturday night partying or hanging out."[33]

Give Seminars and Workshops on Drugs, Sex, Education, Violence, and Racism

We have since realized that the saying "Children are to be seen, not heard" is wrong. As a church we need to talk *with* teenagers, not just preach *to* them about how they may end up dead because of drugs, sex, and violence. Churches need to create safe environments where the teens can come and ask questions about their struggles in making the right choices and decisions. There are experts in the community who can come and address these issues, oftentimes at no cost. In order to be a viable village, we need to have a list of community experts and have seminars and workshops where the teens can come and have conversations about their struggles. We may also find in our churches adults who are "experts," those who have experienced these issues, have addressed them in helpful ways, and have grown because of them. They can share their stories and why and how they managed to be free of such addictions as sex and drugs. A caring village pays attention to the full range of struggles and concerns experienced by its community of parental figures and teenagers and then offers workshops and seminars to try to address these issues.

Be Role Models and Mentors

Many of our teens believe that the best role models are people who make millions of dollars. They forget that some of the best role models are the simple people in their churches and those they meet at the corner store, not people in Hollywood or in sports that they may never meet. The teens need to know that money is not everything, but that values, morals, relationships, belonging to a community, and religious groundedness are what make great role models. The church can easily provide such persons for its teenagers. Teenagers need to understand that most of us are who we are because someone was a role model and a mentor to us. One of the goals of having role models and mentors is for the younger generation to pass on the stories that helped them overcome.

The church can train some of the young adults and adults in the community to mentor the teens. Mentors are dedicated to teaching by action, by appropriately disclosing their own vulnerabilities, and by telling their stories of pain, suffering, joys, and blessings. The mentor is in the public eye of the learner, and mentoring happens in public places. Mentors are committed to praying with and/or for the learner by name in private and in worship services. The relationship calls for accountability of both parties, and the mentor knows that the rituals of caring for the learner go beyond the four walls of the church.

Provide a Place for Teens to "Hang Out"

Churches tend to be more reactive than proactive. When we exist as the "real" village, we provide our youth with a place to "shoot hoops," play indoor games, or watch movies with adult supervision. Some black churches realize that the need to provide safe places for our teens to hang out is critical. There is also a need for after-school programs that churches could easily provide to help with tutoring and homework. Nancy Boyd-Franklin reminds us that this is already happening in many churches. It is not unusual for black churches to provide non-church–related activities such as Boy Scouts and Girl Scouts, basketball teams, youth groups, and so on. Because of limited access to services in many black communities, and deep concerns about the education of black children, many churches have responded by becoming help-centers.[34] But more is needed in this regard.

Reinvest in the Community

There are many in the black community who are financially well-situated. It is important that these individuals "give back" or reinvest in their communities of origin. It is our job as a village to encourage the wealthy to reinvest in our communities so we can invest in the teenagers. A saying goes, "If you find a tortoise on a tree, it did not get there by itself." Any well-to-do black individual did not get rich by himself or herself. An important task for such people is to remember their roots in preparation to pull others up to a higher level. It is high time for the church to fight against the spirit of capitalism and individualism that is destroying the idea of community, that cares less about other humans but more about material possessions. The sense of "I worked very hard for it," "I earned it," "I deserve it," "It's all mine," and "I won't help those in our community of origin who are in need" must be openly countered. In the village we must encourage the spirit of caring, especially for our youth. The church also could create a system of networking with the wealthy so as to help with job searches or to be possible employers for our teens.

Retell the Story—Generation to Generation

Our identities are an interweaving of experiences; personal, family, and community stories; and the Scripture story. These stories that are passed on from generation to generation give us a sense of who we are as individuals and as a church community. The church as village needs to provide (not just from preaching) a place where teenagers can hear the stories of the community and how God has been at work from the past to today. The incorporation of black history in the educational activities is an important means of helping teens develop an inner spiritual center that guides their lives and promotes their envisioning their own unique contributions to society. From the past experiences of black people, our youth discover our history of persons struggling and surviving difficult times, and that the biographies of historic and contemporary figures are replete with lessons about life.[35]

From its African roots, the African American community is a storytelling community. Through story, identities are formed and healing is achieved. Healing cannot be achieved until personal stories of both joy and suffering are told and heard. It is in the stories that people are able to discern where God is at work in their daily lives. Our story becomes complete when seen through the eyes of experience, Scripture, tradition, and reason.

In conclusion, this chapter has tried to present the idea of re-villaging for the African American modern village. It highlighted some of the problems that our youth are facing and gave some pointers on how a few "good enough" parents and the church could help rear our teenagers today. There is great hope in the midst of the struggle.

Questions for Reflection and Discussion

1. To what extent do you rely on and trust your church community to help you in raising your adolescents?

2. What are your feelings about your role as a parental figure in talking with adolescents about sex, drugs, violence, and racism? In what ways have you talked with your teens about sex, drugs, violence, and racism? What help would you seek from your church?

3. As a parental figure, explore your values about sexual activity, the source of these values, and the importance of these values with respect to your teens.

4. What boundaries (curfew, types of friends, and so forth) have you as a parent set for your teens, and how successful have you been in following through with them?

5. In what ways are the strengths and gifts of adolescents identified, affirmed, and used in your home and in the church? What

needs to be done to insure positive feedback, encouragement, and constructive criticism?

6. How important is the church "village" in communicating key values to youth? What would you consider those key values to be? How are these values modeled by church members?

7. What needs to be done to insure that your church village provides an ongoing safe place for youth to come and "hang out" in ways that promote their positive growth and development? What is your role in making this happen?

CHAPTER 6

The Teens Are Watching

Michael T. McQueen

Pay close attention to yourself and to your teaching; continue in these things, for in doing this you will save both yourself and your hearers.

—1 Timothy 4:16

Introduction

In our world today teenagers, especially those who grow up in Christian households, are confused about how to "act properly" within and outside of the church walls. I say this because, in my roles as father of a teenager and preteen and as pastor of a predominantly black church, I "hear" and, more important, "see" what teens are "saying and seeing" concerning the duplicitous roles that their parents and mentors play when it comes to behaving and speaking as Christian adults inside and outside of the church walls. I have sat with teens and listened to them critique everything from the church to their parents to adults to society in general. Their moral stance is found throughout the earlier chapters of this book. Namely, they declare: "The church is full of hypocrites." Added to this accusation, teens make known their observation that "all the churches and preachers want is everybody's money." They are asking, "Why do I need to come to church when I see no difference in the people who attend church versus those who do not attend church?" and "Why do I see so much fighting inside the church?" It is true, as well, that they comment about the deficit of integrity demonstrated by governmental, corporate, and educational leaders in the public sphere of our society.

As indicated in the prologue, our teens have moved past the age of uncritical acceptance of adult authority and life. As adolescents, they are squarely in the stage of scrutiny and evaluation at the very time when they are grappling with their identities, self-worth, self-esteem, spiritual formation, and vocation. Evidence of their critique of adults and their cry for response is found throughout the earlier chapters of this book. The teens are watching us; and a follow-up to what they see and hear is confusion that shows on their faces. They are rightly confused because it appears that we who comprise the Christian church are confused as to how we ourselves are to model a Christian lifestyle and behave in secular society. Our confusion extends to how we are to teach, nurture, and love our teenagers into becoming responsible "whole" spiritual, emotional, social, and caring adults who will one day lead not only our churches but our country and the world. In their adolescence, the youth have become an important moral compass for adults. We must hear their critique and the questions they raise with gratitude and respond with personal behaviors that reflect our commitments as disciples of Jesus Christ.

This chapter presents some reflections that have emerged from my role as black pastor, father, counselor, and confidant. As part of these reflections, I will explore the imperative need for pastors and all other adults to take on the intentional role of models of the Christian lifestyle. I will place further emphasis on what is involved in ensuring the behavior of adults, and conditions that allow this Christian lifestyle, to come alive in consistent ways in order to shape teens' ways of being and behaving as Christians.

The authors of previous chapters have provided important images of black youth from the teens' perspectives, from observations of them, and awareness of critical needs attending their stage of adolescence and unique journey in this country. However, some of the information, especially that in the prologue, bears repeating along with several additional views of black teens today. My presentation of a "picture" of black teens here stems from my view that modeling the Christian lifestyle must not happen in a vacuum or without the youths' knowledge of who they are. Modeling the Christian lifestyle is what we are to carry out in the presence of youth, with their ways of being and acting in the world kept in mind.

It is well to remember that five generations of Americans co-exist in America today, each with its own unique set of experiences begun in a particular time period with a particular group of peers and shaped by the unique social location of individuals and groups. The newest generation of youth differs from other generations—from the adult generations around them. As adults, we are known to wince at the styles of dress and language patterns of our black youth, recoil at their penchant for rap music and hip-hop culture, and grimace at their outspoken accusation: "You're nothing but a hypocrite!" They are part of the generation that George Barna describes as having idiosyncratic values, beliefs, attitudes, and behaviors that will continue to baffle us while, at the same time, presenting to the church a "massive and fertile population for evangelism and discipleship."[1] This generation is larger than and quite different from any generation in history. We need to stop and take notice of the "newest kids on the block," see clearly our differences, and claim the unique contributions we can make in our important task to model the Christian faith.

Looking, Listening, and Learning: Clues for Modeling the Christian Faith

The question may be asked: What must adults be aware of in order for us to take seriously our new or renewed role as models of the Christian faith? In what follows, I will explore answers to the question by focusing on several trends occurring in this new era that have an impact on the lives of teens and call for prompt attention to our role as Christian exemplars.

Clues from Techno-experienced and Spiritually Sensitive Youth

Teens today live in a techno-saturated world. Theirs is the generation in which the Internet, cell phones, DVD players, CD writers, satellite television in schools, and advanced interactive gaming systems burst on the scene. As a group, teens today spend an average of four to six hours per day interacting with mass media in various forms. Ninety-four percent listen to the radio, 91 percent play audiocassettes or compact discs, 89 percent watch television, 69 percent read a magazine, 58 percent read part of a book in a typical day, and 52 use the Internet.[2] And media are generally experienced alone or in isolation.[3] In today's world, teens are overexposed to violence, sex, drugs, and money in such a way that these "forms of entertainment [vices] have become an elixir and opiate for the pain they experience from growing up without the benefit of mentors or both a father and a mother in the home due to the growing incidences of divorce, death, teenage pregnancies, and incarceration."[4]

Amidst the plethora of media images and real-life relationships in the home, community, school, and church, our teens are trying to find identity, meaning, and purpose. For some, the challenge is formidable. Yet it is also true that today's youth are among the most spiritually interested persons in the nation, even though this interest is not necessarily demonstrated in the lifestyles and values they embrace.[5] They see themselves as more "spiritual, optimistic, and ambitious" than their parents' generation.[6] A research report on adolescent spirituality, to which the prologue refers, shows that the importance of religious faith is highest among black adolescents. Recall that 50 percent of black youth identify faith as being very important to them, compared to 33 percent for other ethnic races and 27 percent for white adolescents. Black youth (53 percent) are also more likely than whites (36 percent) to pray daily; and 36 percent of black Protestant youth report being born again, compared to 26 percent of white Protestant youth, 13 percent of Hispanic Protestant youth, and 15 percent of Asian youth.[7] Unfortunately, this positive portrait is not quite how adults view the teens. We tend to magnify the differences between the adult and youth generations to the exclusion of seeing generational differences as opportunities for surprise, awareness, and joy through which to promote the youths' formation of a valued self.

In his book *Relational Refugees*, Edward Wimberly writes that "human identity is formed in a matrix of relationships. We discover ourselves in and through our encounters with others. Our sense of 'me' is dependent on the existence of a 'you.' We can only see our own eyes in the reflection of another's. . . . Adolescents sort through a jumble of messages, both internal and external, as they arrive at some sort of self-understanding. Parents, the church, peers, and teachers all send cues to young people suggesting what they should believe and who they should be."[8] What we want to guard against is that our young people come to believe that what they think is really of no great consequence.[9] Wimberly continues by saying "that some [teenagers/adolescents] get the idea that to be of significance, they have to be someone other than themselves. They strive for affirmation by fitting themselves into someone else's prescribed set of expectations that are often alien to who they truly are. Those who insist on defining themselves by the standards of others will become 'relational refugees.' "[10]

In light of what our teens are seeing, and adults' reticence to see generational differences as opportunities, what is the task of modeling that adults must undertake? I believe that we must demonstrate the meaning of *koinonia* (real community) and, in so doing, not simply forestall our youths' becoming "relational refugees" but present to them an authentic way of being in community for them to emulate. Our youth will learn the meaning of *koinonia* not by what we say it is, but by being part of it or actually experiencing it. In order for this to happen, the church must be a place where persons can come just as they are and share what they have been through in a safe, open, loving, and forgiving environment. The church must be a place where our teenagers can speak the truth in love (Ephesians 4:15), and where they should give all of their cares to the Lord (Psalm 55:22) without fear of rejection or condemnation. The church must be the one place where teenagers can "see" Christians coming together, working together, and crying and laughing together all for the common good. Teenagers are desperately looking for role models and mentors, fathers and mothers who are not afraid to share the "gift of presence" presented in chapter 2. As a central aspect of *koinonia*, this presence is the gift of being available to teens when they are most in need. This is what we, as adults in our churches and homes, must model.

Clues from Teens' Experiences of Mixed Messages

While growing up in the inner city, I often heard my parents and other children's parents say to me and my siblings, "Don't do as I do, but do as I say do." This meant that we were not to emulate how our parents lived their particular lifestyle; rather, we were simply to do as we were told. These mixed signals that we heard and saw meant that our parents' "walk and talk" were not going to be the same and that, regardless of what we saw, we were to obey the spoken word. These same mixed messages are being heard by today's "Mosaic generation." We tell our teenagers to do and be one thing, and yet what they really see is that we adults do not practice what we preach. Chapter 3 drew attention to the reality that many of our teens hear and see adults on Monday through Saturday speak and live in ways that differ from the "spiritual and holy" language and behavior on Sunday mornings. These mixed messages call into question adults' trustworthiness in the eyes of youth.

The issue of trust also emerges from what adults convey, on the one hand, about the value God places on God's people including the youth and, on the other hand, about how adults perceive the youth. Historically, black churches have communicated the message of black people's somebodiness that is automatically given them by God. The affirmation of black youth as children of God and loved by God in sermon material and statements of church members is meant to convey a positive sense of black personhood. However, research shows that teens are aware of adults' perception of them as lazy (84 percent), rude (74 percent), sloppy (70 percent), dishonest (65 percent), friendly (63 percent), intelligent (58 percent), and violent (57 percent).[11]

It is interesting to note that five of the top seven perceptions of adults are negative even though teens do not adjudge themselves in this way. Unfortunately, if teenagers looked at themselves the same way as adults perceive them, then they would suffer from a very low self-image. My concern of this perception of teenagers among adults is that if left unchecked or allowed to fester, then, in the minds and eyes of the beholder, perception will become reality.

What does the youths' perception of trust-defying mixed messages have to say for adults' modeling the Christian faith? Youth learn to trust and how to be trusted when the messages they hear and the behaviors they see are both consistent with the Christian message. Youth learn what authentic faith is through demonstration—not by adults stating a rule for youth to follow, but by adults living *before* youth the meaning of the rule. In fact, by their demonstration of the meaning of Christian living, adults not only build relationships with youth on which youth can count, but also convey understandings of the kind of trust they can count on in their relationship with God.

Similarly, modeling that instills trust must extend beyond words that affirm the value and somebodiness of black youth and beyond inviting youths' reflection on the psalmist's words: "For it was you [God] who formed my inward parts; you knit me together in my mother's womb. I praise you, for I am fearfully and wonderfully made. Wonderful are your works; that I know very well" (Psalm 139:13-14). Trust in adults is built through youths' concrete experience of adults' encouragement and support of them, and the provision of opportunities to develop their gifts and strengths. At the same time, it is essential that adults maintain a sense of trust in our youth. Modeling this trust means adults are careful not to succumb to the current-day tendency to look upon today's youth as morally impaired. Even knowing that adolescents will betray and disappoint the trust of adults by virtue of their testing the limits in their drive for independence, trust by adults gets modeled by willingness to risk, to show patience, and to exercise tough love when needed.

Clues from a Prevailing Fragmentation of Spiritual Life

A few years ago, there was a popular amalgam of letters that was often said and marketed throughout this country. The letters were WWJD, which stood for "What Would Jesus Do?" Often seen on wristbands, T-shirts, pants, and billboards, this combination of letters was designed to remind us of our connection with Jesus Christ and the importance of living after his example. This was supposed to teach and remind Christians that Christianity is to be applied every day of our lives in real-life situations. However, I agree with Drew A. Dyson's critique of the Christian church's inability to help our youth grow spiritually and apply the Christian teachings to their lifestyles: "One of the great disservices done by the modern youth ministry movement and the church at large is the fragmentation of the spiritual life. We have unwittingly perpetuated an understanding of spirituality that separates spiritual formation, justice, worship, service, and fellowship."[12]

Dyson's critique of the church is especially disconcerting in the black church because, in the original African tradition, there is no distinction between the sacred and secular. Adult Christians here in America have underscored this dichotomous lifestyle of sacred and secular by carrying out my earlier mentioned reference to acting one way on Sunday inside the church and another way on Monday through Saturday outside of the church. Our youth are taught by seeing and listening to adult Christians that being Christian is not a way of life or a lifestyle that is to be lived on a day-to-day basis three hundred sixty-five days a year. Rather, it is more like performing a part in a play in which they are actors on stage, or stars in a movie, whereby after the play or movie is over they can go back to doing and being who they "really" are.

The "acting mentality" that members of churches demonstrate to our youth explains how our youth can act one way in church, one way at home, and one way at school, because they have seen their parents and their Christian role models do it so effectively. Our teenagers are learning to "act" their way through church, school, and life; therefore they are not fostering a "real" strong spiritual formation that links and compares their life and lifestyles to that of the ultimate Christian role model, who is Jesus Christ. I agree with Dyson's assertion that "essentially, it is our [the church's] calling to teach and model an integrated understanding of the spiritual life that encompasses inner transformation, community formation, and acts of justice."[13] As a United Methodist pastor, I am reminded of John Wesley, who formed the "Holy Club" in order to actualize his faith and belief in the premise that "one should have holiness of heart and life." For Wesley, living out the Christian faith was not an "act" that only occurred at a certain moment in time, but rather it was a way of life to be lived out every day of one's life.

What does the fragmentation of the spiritual life have to say for the imperative need for adult exemplars of the Christian faith? There is a sense in which the Mosaic generation really needs adults to show and teach them that keeping it real in the Christian life does mean asking, "What Would Jesus Do?" and also appropriating that answer to the everyday situation. I strongly believe that, in the black community, churches are still the spiritual, economic, social, and political fulcrum that enables and empowers our people and communities to grow. Our teenagers should always see us praying and hearing us ask the question "What Would Jesus Do?" before we make decisions inside and outside the church. By our asking this question and modeling the answer, we provide a living foundation that might well spell the difference with regards to teenage pregnancies, HIV/AIDS, homicides, suicides, and drug and alcohol usages.

Peeking into the Future

The apostle Paul wrote, "But this one thing I do: forgetting what lies behind and straining forward to what lies ahead, I press on toward the goal for the prize of the heavenly call of God in Christ Jesus" (Philippians 3:13b-14). As we begin to place the past behind us, with all of our mistakes, misperceptions, and mishaps, and move into the future, what must adults yet be and do that is worthy of the watchful eye of our youth? What is yet needed for Christian adults to fulfill the mandate to send clear messages to our teenagers on what it "really" means to be Christian in the church and in secular society? And what must our churches and families do to help teach, nurture, and love our teenagers in their development toward responsible "whole" spiritual, emotional, social, and loving leaders today and tomorrow?

The Need for a New Paradigm

In her book *Trouble Don't Last Always*, Evelyn L. Parker makes the case for ministry with black youth that centers on emancipatory hope. She states: "Ministry intended to bring about emancipatory hope fosters an integrated spirituality that weaves together both pious and political ideological meanings. Religious belief and social practice are interrelated; they are intertwined. This way of being in the world manifests itself in a variety of forms, including language. Conversely, a fragmented spirituality prohibits the weaving of language, belief, and practice."[14] This means that any real constructive model or paradigm for equipping our teenagers in the upcoming decades will have to be contextual and relevant. It must be from the perspective of our teenagers and not from the perspective of adults.

I believe that one of the mistakes we have made is modeling, witnessing, sharing, and teaching the Christian faith to our teenagers using a paradigm that worked in previous generations but that is insufficient for the Mosaic generation. The past paradigm simply is not relevant for current realities. If we are to successfully help teenagers appropriate their faith in Jesus Christ, and guide them in their decision-making in light of their belief and faith in Jesus Christ, then our churches must take seriously the everyday realities, challenges, temptations, and opportunities youth face. We have to be bold enough to explore and try new methods and modalities without the fear of failure. We have to look inside the church to see if there are any successful Christian models that address the spiritual, social, physical, and emotional needs of our teenagers, and not be afraid to look outside the church to see if there are methods and modalities that we can adapt to our Christian context. For example, in the area of leadership, Lovett H. Weems, Jr. writes: "Most of the best research and writing on leadership in recent years has not been done in the context of the church or not-for-profit institutions. Those in business have done most of this work, followed by those in politics and government."[15] Therefore, just as we have borrowed or adapted secular methods and models of leadership to use in our churches, we also need to look outside the church to explore the possibilities of finding a different look at how we are relating to our teenagers.

Touchstones of a New Paradigm

One interesting paradox that has developed in the past decade is that even though there has been a breakdown in the traditional family unit (father and mother living in the same household with children), George Barna says that family "is [still] a big deal to teenagers, regardless of how they act or what they say."[16] According to Barna, "It is the rare teenager who believes that he or she can lead a fulfilling life without receiving complete acceptance and support from his or her family."[17] I believe that we can begin to construct a viable model for interacting with our teenagers by looking at what Barna has concluded as the top two desired changes teenagers would like to see in their relationships with their fathers and mothers.

According to Barna, the number one desired change that teens desire in their relationships with their fathers is that they spend more time together. With regard to mothers, teens identify their desire for better communication.[18] These two statistics alone suggest the need to create a discipleship model within the church and home, or a community-based initiative outside the church that will address both concerns. Examples of how these needs may be met include the provision of forums such as the intergenerational one presented in the prologue and the quarterly "village" forums given by the Youth Hope-Builders Academy of Interdenominational Theological Center. Forums are designed to bring together parents/guardians and teens for the purposes of supporting "time away" together and engaging them in conversation and communication skills-building. In addition, as the result of these forums, parents and youth together have organized "family rap sessions" on a weekly basis, most often at dinnertime, simply to be together, touch bases, air concerns, and enter into problem-solving.

In response to the overall need for positive adult-to-teen relationships, one suggestion is to develop an adult-to-teen mentoring ministry or group inside or outside the church. Trunell Felder, in the book *In Search of Wisdom: Faith Formation in the Black Church,* presents an example of preparing black males to be mentors.[19]

When preparing for mentoring ministries with adolescent boys or girls, churches or groups should be aware of five types of mentoring relationships presented by researchers Rebecca Saito and Dale Blyth. These types of relationships are important because they are rewarding for both adults and youth:

- **Traditional Relationship:** One adult and one young person form a friendship, with the adult serving as a positive role model;
- **Long-term, Focused Activity Relationship:** One adult is paired with one young person to achieve a particular goal, usually academic;

- **Short-term, Focused Activity Relationship:** This is similar to the previous type, but it involves a shorter commitment;
- **Team Mentoring Relationship:** A family or team forms a friendship with one young person, often from a single-parent family; and
- **Group Mentoring Relationship:** One adult volunteer builds relationships with a group of young people.[20]

The second suggestion is to provide opportunities for teenagers to be heard. Invite them to voice their concerns, challenges, and observations to the adults of the church or community at regularly scheduled intervals and times. I believe it is important that our teenagers have an opportunity to give "voice" within the context of the church, home, and community. Giving voice in the church would necessitate the inclusion of youth in planning for, leading, and evaluating Christian discipleship endeavors. Adding this youth component to the church's model of Christian discipleship would ensure the continuance of a healthy and vital church because of the following reasons:

- It would raise the awareness level of pastors and Christian educators to include youth in the beginning stages of any discipleship planning and implementation model.
- It would invite churches to rethink their current methodologies for including youth in the life of the church.
- It would help churches address age-level ministry (youth), as well as other age-level ministries (from children to older adults), making the discipleship model intergenerational and inclusive.
- It would provide a different approach for churches seeking to increase adult membership at their church, by developing effective discipleship models for youth.[21]

Additional specific considerations in developing effective discipleship models for youth include the following:

- Pastors and Christian educators need to include youth in the beginning stages of planning and implementing models of Christian discipleship. It seems like youth ministry and the attempt to disciple youth in the church is either just an appendage to adult discipleship or an afterthought to adult discipleship. Eugene C. Roehlkepartain in his book, *The Teaching Church: Moving Christian Education to Center Stage,* underscores this point when he indicates that only 48 percent of Christian education programs in most churches address youth needs and interests.[22] Furthermore he writes: "Only 35 percent [of Christian education coordinators] say their programs are innovative and creative, and only 44 percent of coordinators say adults in their congregation place high priority on youth Christian education."[23] Based on these statistics, the author concludes that the problem may be that youth ministry is not a priority in churches.[24] Therefore I believe that by including youth in the beginning stages of planning and implementing a Christian discipleship model will ensure that a "youth's perspective" is included in every phase of the model. One way to address this problem is to establish a Youth Advisory Council consisting primarily of youth and a few adults. This Youth Advisory Council should be consulted whenever any program or ministry in the church is doing anything involving youth members.

- Having a youth component in the Christian discipleship model would encourage churches to rethink their current methodologies for getting youth actively involved in the life of the church. In my opinion, most models of Christian discipleship for youth have not changed or varied much over the past ten years. Yet, the cultural realities (and challenges) facing our youth have changed exponentially, particularly with the advent of the technological and information explosion. Youth today have easier access to much more information than youth ten years ago. In addition to the technological realities facing our youth, there also has been an ever-present need for identity formation. I believe that actively involving our youth in the life of the community of faith will help nurture them and assist them as they attempt to answer the questions "Who am I?" and "Why am I here?"

David Ng, in his article, "Rethinking Youth Ministry," confirms my earlier statement: "The church continues to do youth ministry using models from a different era that don't address the pressing needs of today's youth. . . . [Y]oung people must be integrated into congregational life if youth ministry is to be effective."[25] He continues to explicate how congregations have missed the mark: "Too many youth ministry programs [including discipleship models] are defensive in the sense of seeking to maintain the interest and attendance of the youth. . . . Youth ministry focuses on the fun and entertainment. This approach is futile; fun and entertainment are provided much more professionally and attractively elsewhere in the secular world. Congregations are ill-advised in thinking that to keep young people coming, the youth program must be easy and fun."[26]

Ng concludes by saying, "Having fun and entertainment in youth fellowship is a lower priority than getting help and encouragement to face the demands of life and relationships."[27] Therefore we must replace our outdated methodologies for youth ministry with more relevant and contextual-based programs that address the current issues our youth face (in addition to being fun and entertaining). Attention also needs to focus on the following:

- Having a youth component could assist churches in truly becoming more intergenerational in their approach to ministry. In my opinion, one of the real voids in most churches is the lack of a truly intergenerational focus within them. Most of the church's focus is on individuals between the ages of eighteen to fifty. However, there are many individuals who feel left out of the church and are all alone because there are no ministries specifically designed with them in mind. Eugene C. Roehlkepartain writes that "only 20 percent of congregations adequately promote intergenerational contact. And just 39 percent of youths say their churches do a good or excellent job of helping them get to know adults in the church."[28] One way to address this issue is to begin by identifying the various age groups that exist in a church and then systematically begin to plan and implement models of ministry for that particular age group. Also, Roehlkepartain cites findings from *The Effective Christian Education* study, showing that "intergenerational contact helps young people grow in their faith."[29] Moreover, the study suggests several reasons to encourage intergenerational contact with youth: "First, contact with older adults is more likely to give young people mentors with mature faith. Second, it builds for young people a sense of community in the congregation. Third, intergenerational contact can build mutual respect among the generations. Finally, intergenerational education is another way to build shared experiences of youth and parents, which can open doors for formal and informal faith conversations at home."[30]

- Focusing on a component for youth within a Christian discipleship model can help churches expose and explore the intergenerational needs of the congregation.

- By focusing on a youth component for Christian discipleship, churches may discover new ways to attract adult members. Throughout my ministry, I have seen countless examples of how a family was attracted to and subsequently joined the church due to the exciting and wonderful things that were happening in children's/youth ministry. "According to the *Unchurched American,* 73 percent of unchurched Americans say they want their children to receive religious instruction."[31] Therefore there is a very good possibility that by focusing on ministries for youth, a church can increase the membership to the unchurched.

In my own church, we have chosen to give our teenagers "voice" by promoting their leadership in worship and their own monthly worship service in addition to forming their own usher team, drama ministry, and choir. We also invite their "voices" in the curriculum and subject matter of Bible studies and take them on mission opportunities outside of the church and state. We intentionally have yearly youth and children's lock-ins that are carefully planned by adults and youth to give youth an opportunity to bond and share with adults their concerns and issues. It is amazing to see the difference in morale and self-worth when teenagers voices are welcomed concerning major decisions and functions inside the church. When youth are encouraged and supported in their process of maturation and Christian faith development in a safe, loving, nurturing environment, they will run to the church and view the church as a place where they want to be. It is a place that is *real* and where they can be *real*. I have also seen a direct correlation between those churches that have (in my opinion) growing, dynamic, vital, and community-relevant ministries and the degree to which their youth ministries are growing, dynamic, vital, and intentional about allowing youth to give voice.

Some Concluding Reflections

In conclusion, 1 Timothy 4:16 reminds us to watch our life (what we do) and our doctrine (what we say) closely, "for in doing this [we] will save both [ourselves] and [our] hearers" (Mosaic generation). But even before we do that, we must first remember the words of Jesus in Gethsemane when he reminded his disciples to "Stay awake and pray that you may not come into the time of trial; the spirit indeed is willing, but the flesh is weak"(Matthew 26:41). We must first watch and pray that our spiritual talk will line up with our bodily (physical) walk inside and outside the church. Then we must act faithfully as Christians in our daily lives before God, who knows and loves us and desires that we show and share that love with our youth who seek and need it.

The teenagers are watching. We must always remember that this generation is meticulously watching us to see if we will practice what we preach. They are continually looking for direction and guidance through this maze called life. They are looking for spiritual formation and a sense of being and belonging. They are looking for encouragement, love, and acceptance of who and Whose they are and who they are trying to become. Youth are looking for parental figures to stop trying to vicariously live their lives through them by giving them all of the materialistic things the adults never had growing up. Instead, the one thing young people so desperately need from us is the "gift of presence," or time spent with them alone. Yes, the teens are watching and waiting and hoping that one day soon they will truly understand that we love them with the same love that Jesus Christ gave us, which is agape love. This agape love is unconditional, unearned, unreturned, and given by those who know and remember what it means to be loved when you don't deserve it. So, since we know those in the heavenly realms are already watching the teenagers, let us (adult generation) join them in watching the teens as the teens watch us. Maybe we might just learn something from this hip-hop Mosaic generation.

Questions for Reflection and Discussion

1. How would you describe the youths' perceptions of the adults in your congregation? How would you describe the adults' perceptions of the youth?

2. What importance do you assign to adults' talking the talk and walking the walk in their everyday life? Engage in a conversation with a teen in your family, or a group of youth about the impact of adults' behavior on how they view the church? The Christian faith? Their own commitments to the Christian lifestyle?

3. What needs to change about ways in which adults in your church and community model the Christian faith?

4. What can youth and adults learn from each other about practicing what they profess? What opportunities can be developed for conversations between adults and youth about living the Christian lifestyle, what it means to live it, why it is important to live it, and what is necessary to do to resolve conflicts and questions about it?

Keep It Real:
Claim Hope for Tomorrow

Anne E. Streaty Wimberly

For surely I know the plans I have for you, says the LORD, plans for your welfare and not for harm, to give you a future with hope.

—Jeremiah 29:11

It is fitting that this book should close with some thoughts of black youth. It is appropriate for them to have the "last word." After all, an important theme in the foregoing chapters has been the engagement of youth in conversation, giving them voice, and really hearing what they have to tell us. Moreover, if we consider them to be present and future leaders, then we must invite their opinions and imaginings of the church's ministries. Thus, this epilogue will center on the gifts of insight and queries from ninety-six high school youth who have participated in the Youth Hope-Builders Academy of Interdenominational Theological Center in Atlanta, Georgia, over a two-year period. What appears here resulted from theological reflection sessions into which the youth were invited during the academy's residential program, discussions and presentations of youth during an intergenerational "village" forum of the academy, and an open period of "being real."

Three areas of focus will frame the youths' contributions. First, in light of the hopelessness that many individuals experience today, we invited the youth to reflect on both the necessity and nature of hope in their lives, and the qualities of a hope-builder. We wanted to know the thoughts they have about the concept of hope and hope-building and the extent of their personalized sense of its relevance and meaning for them and others. Second, churches often tell our academy staff that they want answers to their malaise in creating welcoming environments for youth and ministries that "keep it real." It is clear that they have not done it because the vision has eluded them and the ingenuity of the youth has remained untapped. On this basis, we asked all of the youth attending a forum entitled "The Youth-Friendly Church" to take the role of teacher and provide some "food" for thought and action. Finally, in light of our awareness that black youth often hold within them burning questions that come up in the "heat" of their daily journey, we invited them to share some of them. What emerged from the youth was a powerful testament to their ability and delight in "keeping it real," and not simply the clear presence of hope, but their willingness to share it for the sake of their own and the community's future.

Claiming Hope

To the youth in the Youth Hope-Builders Academy, hope is something that is necessary, real, and concrete and that seems to develop in the midst of hardship, quandary, and wonderment about what lies ahead. But their description of hope also points to what our black forbears called "going on to see what the end will be." Clearly, the youths' understanding of hope and hope-building is a gift to us all.

The Nature and Meaning of Hope

The most powerful description of the necessity of hope was given by a teen who simply said: "You have to have the drive that keeps you going when all odds are against you. For me, that is hope." The responses of other youth to the nature and meaning of hope in their lives formed around four different themes. Their responses appear as follows:

HOPE AS BELIEF OR FAITH IN GOD AND SELF

- Hope is believing there is a higher power that you can turn to in times of need.

- Hope is the will to keep faith in something and believe that everything will turn out okay. It is belief that you can come out of any hardship. When you have faith, you believe that something can be accomplished even though it seems out of reach or impossible. Hope is faith, faith is believing, believing is achieving, and achieving is succeeding. Hope is believing in the unseen. Hope is the presence of courage to believe. It is knowing that you can reach a goal. Hope is having faith in something you might not have any control over; and even though you might not know how it is going to turn out in the end, you know it will turn out for the best. Hope is believing you can make a difference.

- Hope means always believing in God and letting God take control; it is trust! With hope, you put it all in God's hands and trust and believe in whatever the outcome. It is a way back to God in a trying situation.

- Hope means trusting yourself. It is having faith in me.

HOPE AS VISION, GOAL, EXPECTATION, DESIRE, OR OPPORTUNITY

- I would describe hope as a dream/vision towards the future. Hope is the ability to see a positive light in a seemingly bleak situation.

- Hope is stronger than a wish; it's a goal that you know you can achieve. It is that something pushing inside of you toward the future after you had already given up.

- In essence, hope is expecting good to come out of a challenging or impossible situation. Hope means no matter how hard something is, there is still that chance of pulling through. Hope means that there is still an opportunity for me to make a difference. It is having something to hold on to, to look forward to when you are down. It is overcoming destructive temptations and seeing the future as worthy of attaining.

HOPE AS MOTIVATION, EFFORT, STRIVING, OR DETERMINATION

- Hope means not giving up, but striving for a goal.

- Hope is everything to me—it is the key that can open any door; but you have to put a little effort behind it to turn the lock. Hope is the will to carry on even if you are going in a storm. It is believing God is with you and fighting your battles.

- Hope is a strong type of determination—determination on behalf of God.

- Hope is never-ending determination. It means you can't fail.

HOPE AS SPIRITUAL OR INTUITIVE AWARENESS
AND AS A WAY OF BEING

- Hope means being a partaker of a certain spiritual feeling that can be shared with all. It is the feeling that you can do something no matter what the task.

- Hope is an awareness of a spiritual presence that can guide you.

- Hope is being there for those in need.

The Person and Qualities of the Hope-builder

The youth considered the hope-builder to be a leader, a supporter, a motivator, a visionary, and a strong believer. Their specific descriptions are as follows:

- A hope-builder is a leader who guides others in finding out who they are. The leader is purposeful, courageous, fearless, determined, creative, special, distinctive, empowering, motivating, God-fearing, trustworthy, honest, intellectually gifted, caring, compassionate, diverse, fun, understanding, spiritual, curious, helpful, outspoken, articulate, and respectful. The hope-builder is one who sees one's own leadership abilities and the leadership abilities of others. The hope-builder is a leader who never gives up. The person believes in the self through good and bad and shows others how to survive in a bad situation.

- A hope-builder is a supporter who uplifts and encourages others in the community and helps them to explore life's possibilities.

- A hope-builder is a motivator—someone who inspires others to achieve ultimate goals. This person has hope within the self and instills it in others. The hope-builder brings life into the environment or world. A hope-builder is able to inspire others through dedicated, responsible, anointed, noble, nourishing, and extraordinary action.

- A hope-builder is a visionary—someone who is able to look ahead on the positive aspects of life, leading others forward, but is also willing to follow.

- A hope-builder is someone who has a strong Christian faith and is able to exhibit Christian life characteristics. A hope-builder has a foundation of faith. The hope-builder may come across an obstacle, but will still overcome the situation because she or he believes things will change.

Giving Advice on the Youth-friendly Church

At a forum on "The Youth-friendly Church," the youth participants met in small groups to develop their "manifesto" of recommendations for churches to consider and act on in order to be an environment that "keeps it real" for the youth. The youths' proposal included ten points:

- Let us know that we are needed. Acknowledge us.

- Take seriously the idea of youth representation at all levels. Allow us to have leadership in worship. Let us participate on church boards. Have a youth Sunday, but go beyond that. Give us prime-time exposure.

- Allow forums, rap sessions, town hall meetings, and panels. Allow for our voices. Risk a realistic discussion of issues. Let us talk to adults about topics such as drugs and sex. Allow us more freedom of expression. Try to understand what we are going through. Be considerate and open-minded.

- Pay attention to our likes and dislikes. Have activities like movies, lock-ins, step teams, rap, holy hip-hop, comics.

- We need respect from adults. It is important to give respect in order to earn respect.

- Criticism is not always helpful.

- Make sermons more applicable to our lives. Preach life!

- Help us gain more knowledge of what Christ has for us.

- Be open to more energetic music. Make the Scripture come alive. Let us act it out. Let the words become flesh.

- Let us come as we are. Let us wear casual dress.

Raising Burning Questions

In the Youth Hope-Builders Academy, we discovered that high school youth think deeply about issues of faith, want to share the burning questions that come to them, and need opportunities to explore the issues as means of forming, affirming, and deepening their faith. The intent here is not to provide answers to the questions the youth raised, although a role of the academy is to engage youth in exploring responses. Our purpose is simply to present some of the questions as means of demonstrating the depth of teens' thoughts to which they want to give voice:

- Who am I? What does it mean to *really know* who I am?

- Is the creation story a myth?

- How do we really know what is told to us about God and the Bible? Why do we believe what we do?

- What is predestination? If God knows every hair on our heads and already knows everything that is going to happen to us and everything we will do, then why should we be concerned about our lives?

- There is talk about the man as the head in a marriage or in society. Is that true? If God created men and women equally and God is a spirit, why do we constantly refer to God as a man?

- The Bible says that we shall not kill. It also says that we are what we think. If we believe in capital punishment, are we guilty of sin?

- If we are responsible for creating the kingdom of heaven here on earth, why would/should we exclude people who are gay or lesbian?

- As a black/African American community, do we really possess a sense of accountability and/or obligation to everyone and everything within and around our community? How should we or can we exercise this sense of community responsibility or obligation?

Questions for Reflection and Discussion

1. Explore your understandings of hope and hope-building. What qualities would you say are important for a hope-builder? Enter into conversation with a teenager or a group of youth about the nature and meanings of hope and hope-building.

2. What are the signs of a youth-friendly environment in your church? What qualities of a youth-friendly church given by youth in this chapter already happen in your church? What must your church do to improve the environment for youth in order to "keep it real?"

3. What questions are the youth in your church or home raising? What opportunities are there for them to offer their questions and explore the answers? Enter into conversation with a teen or a group of youth to explore their questions and to search for answers.

4. What answers would you give to the questions raised in this chapter? Explore possible answers in Bible commentaries, library books, and other resources.

Contributors

Daniel O. Black, Ph.D., is associate professor, Department of English at Clark Atlanta University, Atlanta, Georgia. He is also the youth choir director at First Iconium Baptist Church, and Baba (Swahili for "father") of the Ndugu and Nzigha Rites of Passage Society.

Philip Dunston, Ph.D., is assistant professor and program director, Department of Religion and Philosophy at Clark Atlanta University. He is also program co-coordinator of the Youth Hope-Builders Academy of Interdenominational Theological Center, and pastor of Friendship Baptist Church in Appling, Georgia.

Maisha I. Handy, Ph.D., is assistant professor of Christian education and co-program coordinator of the Youth Hope-Builders Academy at Interdenominational Theological Center, Atlanta, Georgia. She is also youth ministry director at First Iconium Baptist Church, Atlanta, Georgia.

Annette R. Marbury is a mother, grandparent, lifelong church member, teacher, and leader in ministries with children and youth in United Methodist churches. She is currently a member of Kelley Chapel United Methodist Church in Decatur, Georgia.

Herbert R. Marbury, Ph.D., is assistant professor of religion and university chaplain at Clark Atlanta University, Atlanta, Georgia. He is an ordained United Methodist minister, and has served as an Exploration Group leader in the Youth Hope-Builders Academy of Interdenominational Theological Center.

Michael T. McQueen, D.Min., is adjunct professor of Christian education at Interdenominational Theological Center, Atlanta, Georgia. He is the senior pastor of Ousley United Methodist Church in Lithonia, Georgia, and serves as the president of the Advisory Board of the Youth Hope-Builders Academy of Interdenominational Theological Center.

Tapiwa Mucherera, Ph.D., is associate professor of pastoral care and counseling and chairperson of the Pastoral Care and Counseling Department at Asbury Seminary, Wilmore, Kentucky. He is an ordained United Methodist minister in the Zimbabwe Annual Conference and has been a Youth Hope-Builders Academy forum presenter.

Elizabeth J. Walker, Th.D., is an adjunct professor of pastoral care and counseling at Interdenominational Theological Center, Atlanta, Georgia. She is also a licensed marriage and family therapist in the state of Georgia and a staff counselor at the Care and Counseling Center of Georgia in Atlanta. She has been a Youth Hope-Builders Academy forum presenter.

Anne E. Streaty Wimberly, Ph.D., is professor of Christian education and director of the Youth Hope-Builders Academy at Interdenominational Theological Center, Atlanta, Georgia. She is also the Principal Investigator of the Faith Journey Program at the Interdenominational Theological Center. Her recent publications include *In Search of Wisdom: Faith Formation in the Black Church; Nurturing Faith and Hope: Worship as a Model for Christian Education; and Soul Stories: African American Christian Education,* revised edition.

Notes

Prologue

1. The proverb is found in Julia Stewart, *African Proverbs and Wisdom* (Secaucus, NJ: Carol Publishing Group, 1998), p. 86.

2. The hope-bearing effort described here resembles Joyce West Stevens' delineation of a social work principle. The principle "involves the efforts of the practitioner to strengthen the participant's sense of hope and hardiness to realize present and future personal goals." Stevens suggests two primary techniques including, first, making use of social and environmental circumstances to help adolescents in their self-creation of personal meaning and wisdom and, second, using techniques that include visual imagery that enables adolescents to become more future-oriented. See Joyce West Stevens, *Smart and Sassy: The Strengths of Inner-city Black Girls* (New York: Oxford University Press, 2002), p. 177.

3. See Lawrence N. Jones, "The Black Churches: A New Agenda," in Milton C. Sernett, ed., *Afro-American Religious History: A Documentary Witness* (Durham, NC: Duke University Press, 1985), pp. 494-97; C. Eric Lincoln and Lawrence H. Mamiya, *The Black Church in the African American Experience* (Durham, NC: Duke University Press, 1990), pp. 309-45.

4. See Sharon L. Nichols and Thomas L. Good, *America's Teenagers—Myths and Realities: Media Images, Schooling, and the Social Costs of Careless Indifference* (Mahwah, NJ: Lawrence Erlbaum Associates, Publishers, 2004), p. 48.

5. Ibid., pp. 39, 243.

6. See George Barna, *Real Teens: A Contemporary Snapshot of Youth Culture* (Ventura, CA: Regal Books, 2001), pp. 48-49; Nichols and Good, *America's Teenagers—Myths and Realities*, pp. 37-39, 99.

7. See ibid., pp. 239, 243-45; U.S. Census Bureau, "The Black Population in the United States: March 2002" (Washington, DC: Department of Commerce, Economics and Statistics Administration, U.S. Census Bureau, April 2003), p. 6.

8. Kirk A. Astroth, "Are Youth at Risk?" *Journal of Extension*, vol. 31(3), Fall 1993. See p. 2 of printed version online: http://www.joe.org.

9. Christian Smith, et al., "Mapping American Adolescent Subjective Religiosity and Attitudes of Alienation Toward Religion: A Research Report," *Sociology of Religion*, Spring 2003. See pp. 7-8 of printed version online: http://www.findarticles.com.

10. Ibid., pp. 7-8; Barna, *Real Teens*, pp. 15-16; Richard Land, "Barna: A View of the Mosaic Generation (Born from 1984 to 2002)," an interview with George Barna. See p. 5 online: http://www.pastors.com.

11. Beverly Daniel Tatum, *"Why Are All the Black Kids Sitting Together in the Cafeteria?" And Other Conversations About Race* (New York: Basic Books, 1997), pp. 52-53.

12. Ibid.

13. bell hooks writes about engaged pedagogy, which encompasses an engaged form of education focused on connecting teaching and learning with the overall life experiences of those being educated. See bell hooks, *Teaching to Transgress: Education as the Practice of Freedom* (New York: Vintage Books, 1994), pp. 23-24.

14. See Stevens, *Smart and Sassy*, p. 163.

15. Cornel West, *Race Matters* (New York: Vintage Books, 1994), pp. 23-24.

16. Ibid., p. 24.

17. Ibid.

18. Stevens, *Smart and Sassy*, p. 91.

19. Ibid., p. 92.

20. Ibid.

21. Nichols and Good, *America's Teenagers*, p. 10.

22. Nichols and Good present findings of a 1997 study showing 67 percent of adults used the indicated negative adjectives. Moreover, the proportion using these adjectives increased to 74 percent in a 1999 study. See ibid., p. 11.

23. See Andrew Billingsley, *Climbing Jacob's Ladder: The Enduring Legacy of African American Families* (New York: Simon & Schuster, 1992).

24. See Andrew Billingsley, *Mighty Like a River: The Black Church and Social Reform* (New York: Oxford University Press, 1999).

25. Jawanza Kunjufu, *Restoring the Village, Values, and Commitment: Solutions for the Black Family* (Chicago: African American Images, 1996), p. 143.

26. Ibid., p. 152.

27. Jack O. Balswick and Judith K. Balswick, *The Family: A Christian Perspective on the Contemporary Home* (Grand Rapids, MI: Baker Books, 1999), pp. 332-33.

28. Ibid., p. 333.

29. Ibid., p. 338.

30. See ibid., pp. 340-41.

31. Astroth, "Are Youth at Risk?" p. 2.

32. Eugene H. Peterson, *Like Dew Your Youth: Growing Up with Your Teenager* (Grand Rapids, MI: William B. Eerdmans Publishing Company, 2000), p. 5.

33. Ibid., pp. 6-7.

34. Ibid., p. 8.

35. See J'Anne Ellsworth, "Today's Adolescent: Addressing Existential Dread" (Gale Group, 2001). See p. 2 of printed version online: http://www.findarticles.com.

36. Peterson, *Like Dew Your Youth*, p. 63.

37. See ibid., p. 64.

38. Ibid.

39. Ibid.

40. Ibid., p. 69.

41. Asa G. Hilliard, III, *The Maroon Within Us: Selected Essays on African American Community Socialization* (Baltimore, MD: Black Classic Press, 1995), p. 138.

42. Ibid., p. 138.

43. Ibid.

1. The Gift of the Youth

1. A word of gratitude goes to Victor Cyrus-Franklin, a third-year seminarian at the Interdenominational Theological Center. He offered his years of experience in youth ministry and was a particularly helpful dialogue partner, sharing clear and valuable insight.

2. John 6:1-15.

3. Leon Morris, *The Gospel According to John: The New International Commentary on the New Testament* (Grand Rapids, MI: 1971), p. 344. The word can refer to anyone from a young boy to age seventeen. See the LXX Genesis 37:30 where the word is used to describe Joseph.

4. The poem, entitled "Names," appears online: http:www.geocities.com/TheTropic/Shores/3456/names.html.

5. S. Miriam Dunson, ed., *Facing Forward in Older Adult Ministry* (Louisville, KY: Geneva Press, 1999), p. 5.

6. Edward A. Loder, *Building an Intergenerational Church* (Louisville, KY: Westminster John Knox, 1999), p. 2.

7. Ibid., p. 6.

8. Some of the most insightful social critiques are found in music of young people. Amazingly, the music industry and popular culture hungrily consume the voices of our young people in rap music. Sadly, these voices oftentimes never reach the church.

9. Dean Borgman, *When Kumbaya Is Not Enough: A Practical Theology for Youth Ministry* (Peabody, MA: Hendrickson, 1999), p. xiii.

10. Fording shows how the Protestant right often colludes with the Republican right to reinforce poverty in certain areas, particularly black communities. See Richard D. Fording, "Laboratories of Democracy or Symbolic Politics," in Sanford F. Schram, Joe Soss, and Richard Fording, eds., *Race and the Politics of Welfare Reform* (Ann Arbor, MI: University of Michigan Press, 2003), pp. 84-87.

11. Michael Card, *Basin and Towel* (Brentwood, TN: Sparrow Records, 1994).

12. Howard Thurman, *The Creative Encounter* (Richmond, IN: Friends United Press, 1954), pp. 26-27.

13. Henri J. M. Nouwen, *With Open Hands* (Notre Dame, IN: Ave Maria Press, 1998), pp. 91-92.

14. Ibid., p. 92.

15. Keith Boykin, *One More River to Cross: Black and Gay in America* (New York: Anchor Books, 1996), pp. 131-32.

16. Ibid., p. 131.

17. The youth made specific references to the war in Iraq.

18. From the song "Ordinary People," by Danniebelle Hall.

2. A Matter of Discovery

1. Various aspects of Erikson's views are found in Erik Erikson, *Childhood and Society*, second edition (New York: Norton & Company, 1964); Erik Erikson, *Identity, Youth, and Crises* (New York: W.W. Norton and Company, 1968).

2. Carole Wade, *Psychology* (New York: HarperCollins College Publishers, 1996), p. 459.

3. Ibid.

4. Stevens, *Smart and Sassy*, p. 121.

5. Ibid., pp. 121-22. Stevens draws on P. S. Fry, "The Development of Personal Meaning and Wisdom," in P. S. Fry, ed., *The Human Quest for Meaning* (Mahwah, NJ: Lawrence Erlbaum Associates, Publishers, 1998), p. 95.

6. Stevens makes the point that "a belief in the spiritual essence of life transforms the self in such a way that living is more than survival; life becomes valued, principled, joyful, and hopeful." See Stevens, *Smart and Sassy*, xvi.

7. See ibid., p. 91.

8. Ibid., p. 90.

9. Ibid.

10. Bakari Kitwana, *The Hip Hop Generation: Young Blacks and the Crisis in African American Culture* (New York: BasicCivitas Books, 2002), p. xxi.

11. Stevens, *Smart and Sassy*, p. 179.

12. Ibid.

13. Blake J. Neff, "Communications and Relationships," in Donald Ratcliff and James A. Davies, eds., *Handbook of Youth Ministry* (Birmingham, AL: Religious Education Press, 1991), p. 171.

14. See R. Alan Culpepper, "The Gospel of Luke: Introduction, Commentary, and Reflections," in *The New Interpreter's Bible*, vol. 9 (Nashville: Abingdon Press, 1995), p. 304.

15. Ibid., p. 305.

16. See Anne Streaty Wimberly, "The Violence of Racism, the Strategy of Empowerment: Relational Hope and Co-action with Black Youth," *Black Theology: An International Journal* 1(1), November 2002: 53-66 (62).

17. Ibid.

18. Ibid.

19. Ibid.

20. *Merriam Webster's New Collegiate Dictionary*, Tenth edition (Springfield, MA: Merriam-Webster, 1983), p. 234.

21. Lincoln and Mamiya, *The Black Church in the African American Experience*, p. 398.

22. Wimberly, "The Violence of Racism," p. 63.

23. Ibid., p. 64.

24. Ibid.

25. The list also builds on a paradigm of advocacy appearing in Wimberly, "The Violence of Racism," pp. 65-66.

26. Mbiti's philosophical views are described in Reginald Jones, *Black Psychology* (Berkeley, CA: Cobb & Henry Publishers, 1991), p. 48.

27. Ibid., p. 49.

3. Getting Real

1. bell hooks talks about engaged pedagogy in *Teaching to Transgress*, p. 19.

2. West, *Race Matters* , pp. 23-24.

3. Ibid., p. 24.

4. Ibid.

5. Wade Nobles, "Africanity: Its Role in Black Families," in Robert Staples, ed., *The Black Family: Essays and Studies* (Belmont, CA: Wadsworth, 1978), p. 22.

6. Anne E. Streaty Wimberly and Maisha I. Handy, "Conversations on Word and Deed: Forming Wisdom Through Female Mentoring," in Anne E. Streaty Wimberly and Evelyn L. Parker, eds., *In Search of Wisdom: Faith Formation in the Black Church* (Nashville: Abingdon Press, 2002), p. 112.

7. Jawanza Kunjufu, *A Talk with Jawanza: Critical Issues in Educating African American Youth* (Chicago: African American Images, 1989), p. 63.

8. See Edward Wimberly, Anne E. Streaty Wimberly, and Annie Grace Chingonzo, "Pastoral Counselling, Spirituality, and the Recovery of the Village Functions: African and African-American Correlates in the Practice of Pastoral Care and Counselling," in John Foskett and Emmanuel Lartey, eds., *Spirituality and Culture in Pastoral Care and Counselling: Voices from Different Contexts* (Cardiff, United Kingdom: Cardiff Academic Press, 2004), pp. 16-17.

9. See chapter 3 in Robert M. Franklin, *Another Day's Journey: Black Churches Confronting the American Crisis* (Minneapolis: Fortress Press, 1997).

10. In his essay, William Myers argues the importance of an African-centered hermeneutic and the psycho-spiritual costs of blacks interpreting the Bible without it. See William H. Myers, "The Hermeneutical Dilemma of the African American Biblical Student," in Cain Hope Felder, ed., *Stony the Road We Trod: African American Biblical Interpretation* (Minneapolis: Fortress Press, 1991), pp. 40-56.

11. Yolanda Y. Smith, "Forming Wisdom Through Cultural Rootedness," in Wimberly and Parker, *In Search of Wisdom*, p. 44.

12. The symbol is that of a bird named sankofa in the Akan tradition in Africa. The bird has a long neck stretching back toward its tail, stands on three steps, and represents the idea of going back to the African ancestors to learn what lies ahead. See Smith, "Forming Wisdom Through Cultural Rootedness," p. 49. In her use of the symbol, Smith draws on Nsenga Warfield-Coppock, *Adolescent Rites of Passage*, vol. 1, Afrocentric Theory and Applications (Washington, DC: Baobab Associates, 1990), p. 8.

13. In discussing the pervasive sense of despair in black communities, West defines nihilism as "the lived experience of coping with a life of horrifying meaninglessness, hopelessness, and [most important] lovelessness." See West, *Race Matters*, p. 14.

14. Malidome Patrice Somé, *The Healing Wisdom of Africa: Finding Life Purpose Through Nature, Ritual, and Community* (New York: Penguin Putnam, 1998), p. 22.

15. Ibid., p. 27.

16. Ibid.

17. Ibid., p. 23.

18. Ibid., p. 24.

19. Ibid., p. 28

20. Ibid., p. 32.

21. Harley Atkinson, *Ministry with Youth in Crisis* (Birmingham, AL: Religious Education Press, 1997), p. 181.

22. Ibid., p. 183.

23. Ibid., pp. 170-211.

24. See Ronald L. Kotesky, "Adolescence as a Cultural Invention," in Donald Ratcliff and James A Davies, eds., *The Handbook of Youth Ministry* (Birmingham, AL: Religious Education Press, 1991), pp. 58-63.

25. Stevens, *Smart and Sassy*, pp. 141-45.

26. Paulo Freire, *Education for Critical Consciousness* (New York: Continuum, 1973), p. 105.

27. Ibid.

28. See Tom Beaudoin, *Virtual Faith: The Irreverent Spiritual Quest of Generation X* (San Francisco: Jossey-Bass Publishers, Inc. 1998).

29. See ibid., p. 19.

30. Freire, *Educating for Critical Consciousness*, p. 102.

31. Smith, "Forming Wisdom Through Cultural Rootedness," p. 110.

4. Called to Parent: Parenting as Ministry

1. Peterson, *Like Dew Your Youth*, p. 1.

2. Ibid., p. 4.

3. Ibid.

4. A commentator describes procreation in the following terms: "Procreation is both God's gift and his command, and man's task from creation is to fill the earth and subdue it, to join in God's will for order." See George A. Buttrick, *The Interpreter's One-volume Commentary on the Bible* (Nashville: Abingdon Press, 1990), p. 4.

5. See Ronald E. Clements, "The Book of Deuteronomy: Introduction, Commentary, and Reflections," in *The New Interpreter's Bible*, vol. 2 (Nashville: Abingdon Press, 1998), pp. 340-45.

6. Niara Sudarkasa, "Interpreting the African Heritage in Afro-American Family Organization," in Harriette Pipes McAdoo, ed., *Black Families* (Thousand Oaks, CA: Sage Publications, 1997), pp. 37-53.

7. Ibid.

8. Jualynne Dodson, "Conceptualizations of Black Families," in McAdoo, *Black Families*, p. 27.

9. See ibid., pp. 23-36.

10. Ibid.

11. See Marie F. Peters, "Parenting in Black Families with Young Children: A Historical Perspective," in McAdoo, *Black Families*, pp. 211-24.

12. Billingsley, *Climbing Jacob's Ladder*, pp. 17-23.

13. Wade W. Nobles, "African-American Family Life: An Instrument of Culture," in McAdoo, *Black Families*, pp. 77-86.

14. Robert Joseph Taylor, et al., "Recent Demographic Trends in African American Family Structure," in Robert Joseph Taylor, et al., eds., *Family Life in Black America* (Thousand Oaks, CA: Sage Publications, 1997), pp. 14-62. U.S. Census Bureau data show that in 2002 43 percent of black people had never married, and 35 percent were not currently married. See U.S. Census Bureau, "The Black Population in the United States: March 2002," p. 3.

15. Taylor, et al., "Recent Demographic Trends in African American Family Structure," p. 16.

16. In 2001, the poverty rate was 23 percent for blacks, compared to 12 percent for the total population and 8 percent for non-Hispanic whites. See U.S. Census Bureau, "The Black Population in the United States: March 2002," p. 3.

17. Christopher G. Ellison, "Religious Involvement and the Subjective Quality of Family Life Among African Americans," in Taylor, et al., *Family Life in Black America*, pp. 117-31.

18. Ibid., p. 119.

19. Paulette Moore Hines, "The Family Life Cycle of African American Families," in Betty Carter and Monica McGoldrick, eds., *The Expanded Family Life Cycle: Individual, Family, and Social Perspectives* (Boston: Allyn and Bacon Publishers, 1999), pp. 327-45.

20. William C. Nichols, *Treating People in Families: An Integrative Framework* (New York: Guilford Press, 1996), pp. 70-71.

21. Ibid.

22. Edward P. Wimberly, *Pastoral Counseling of African American Marriages and Families* (Louisville: Westminster John Knox Press, 1997), p. 60.

23. Nichols, *Treating People in Families*, pp. 194-95.

5. Hope in the Midst of Struggle

1. Shona is a name for both an African ethnic group and the language they speak. Shonas are mainly found in Zimbabwe but, due to arbitrary boundaries set by colonialists, some are found in neighboring countries.

2. Tapiwa N. Mucherera, *Pastoral Care from a Third World Perspective: A Pastoral Theology of Care for the Urban Contemporary Shona in Zimbabwe* (New York: Peter Lang Publishers, 2001), p. 54.

3. See Nichols and Good, *America's Teenagers—Myths and Realities*, pp. 15-16.

4. References to those who parent the youth include biological parents, adopted parents, foster parents, grandparents, and other kin who are raising children.

5. Richard K. James and Burl E. Gilliland, *Crisis Intervention Strategies* (Pacific Grove, CA: Brooks/Cole Thompson Learning, 2001), p. 520.

6. Nichols and Good, *America's Teenagers*, p. 19.

7. Nancy Boyd-Franklin and A. J. Franklin, *Boys into Men: Raising Our African American Teenage Sons* (New York: Dutton Books, 2001), p. 25.

8. Nichols and Good, *America's Teenagers*, p. 7.

9. Ibid., pp. 99-100.

10. Ibid., p. 100.

11. Ibid., p. 101.

12. Nichols and Good cite a 2003 study showing that the "overwhelming majority of both parents (88%) and teens (88%) reported that sexual health issues (such as STDs, HIV, and pregnancy) were the biggest problems above sexual violence or other physical violence; drug use; discrimination because of race, ethnicity, or sexual orientation; excessive drinking or smoking; or depression or other mental illness." See ibid., p. 107.

13. Drs. Edward Wimberly and Tapiwa N. Mucherera presented the idea of re-villaging in an unpublished paper at the Fourth Congress of the African Association of Pastoral Studies and Counseling in Yaounde Cameroon, West Africa, July 27, 2001.

14. Nancy Boyd-Franklin, *Black Families in Therapy: Understanding the African American Experience*, Second edition (New York: Guilford Press, 2003), pp. 127-28.

15. Jay Kesler, *Raising Responsible Kids: Ten Things You Can Do Now to Prepare for a Lifetime of Independence* (Brentwood, TN: Wolgemuth & Hyatt, Publishers, 1991), p. 99.

16. Boyd-Franklin and Franklin, *Boys into Men*, p. 56.

17. Atkinson, *Ministry with Youth in Crisis*, pp. 88-89.

18. James and Gilliland, *Crisis Intervention Strategies*, p. 528.

19. Atkinson, *Ministry with Youth in Crisis*, p. 86. Atkinson draws on data from a study by Sebine found in the chapter by Gary Dausey, "Communication Killers," in Jay Kesler, ed., *Parents and Teenagers* (Wheaton, IL: Victor Books, 1988), p. 226.

20. Ibid.

21. Ibid.

22. Jeffries J. McWhirter, et al., *At-Risk Youth: A Comprehensive Response—For Counselors, Teachers, Psychologists, and Human Services Professionals*, Third edition (Belmont, CA: Brooks/Cole Publishers, 2003), pp. 141-42.

23. Ibid., p. 140.

24. Bruce Cook, *The Big Talk Book: Parents, Teens, and Sex* (Marietta, GA: Choosing the Best, LLC, 2002).

25. Kesler, *Raising Responsible Kids*, p. 133.

26. See Atkinson, *Ministry with Youth in Crisis*, pp. 95-100.

27. This dramatization is suggested in Chris Jackson, *Straight Talk on Tough Topics: A Discussion Guidebook for Today's Afrikan-American Youth* (Grand Rapids, MI: Zondervan Publishing House, 1996), p. 50.

28. Boyd-Franklin and Franklin, *Boys into Men*, pp. 27, 32-33.

29. Ibid., p. 25.

30. Man Keung Ho, *Minority Children and Adolescents in Therapy* (Thousand Oaks, CA: Sage Publications, 1992), p. 79.

31. Boyd-Franklin, *Black Families in Therapy*, pp. 130-31.

32. Man Keung Ho, *Minority Children and Adolescents in Therapy*, p. 78.

33. Boyd-Franklin and Franklin, *Boys into Men*, p. 54.

34. Boyd-Franklin, *Black Families in Therapy*, p. 131.

35. Boyd-Franklin and Franklin, *Boys into Men*, p. 57.

6. The Teens Are Watching

1. Barna, *Real Teens*, pp. 15-16.

2. Ibid., p. 26.

3. Nichols and Good, *America's Teenagers—Myths and Realities*, pp. 37-38.

4. Barna, *Real Teens*, p. 48.

5. See The Barna Update, "Teens Change Their Tune Regarding Self and Church," April 23, 2002. Printed at http://www.barna.org.

6. Nichols and Good, *America's Teenagers—Myths and Realities*, p. 13.

7. Christian Smith, et. al., "Mapping American Adolescent Subjective Religiosity and Attitudes of Alienation Toward Religion: A Research Report," *Sociology of Religion*, Spring 2003. See pp. 7-8 on the reprinted version online: http://www.looksmart.com.

8. Edward P. Wimberly, *Relational Refugees: Alienation and Reincorporation in African American Churches and Communities* (Nashville: Abingdon Press, 2000), p. 63.

9. Ibid.

10. Ibid., pp. 63-64.

11. Ibid., p. 55.

12. Drew A. Dyson, *Faith-forming Junior High Ministry: Beyond Pizza 101* (Nashville: Abingdon Press, 2003), p. 39.

13. Ibid.

14. Evelyn L. Parker, *Trouble Don't Last Always: Emancipatory Hope Among African American Adolescents* (Cleveland: Pilgrim Press, 2003), pp. 35-36.

15. Lovett H. Weems, Jr., *Church Leadership: Vision, Team, Culture, and Integrity* (Nashville: Abingdon Press, 1993), p. 23.

16. Barna, *Real Teens*, p. 68.

17. Ibid.

18. Ibid., pp. 79-71.

19. See Trunell D. Felder, "Counsel from Wise Others: Forming Wisdom Through Male Mentoring," in Wimberly and Parker, *In Search of Wisdom*, pp. 89-107.

20. Rick Lawrence, *Trendwatch: Insights That Fuel Authentic Youth Ministry* (Loveland, CO: Group Press, 2000), p. 107.

21. Michael T. McQueen, "Educating for Christian Discipleship: A Comparative Approach to Contextual Planning and Implementation" (D.Min. dissertation, Atlanta: Interdenominational Theological Center, 2002), pp. 74-75.

22. Eugene C. Roehlkepartain, *The Teaching Church: Moving Christian Education to Center Stage* (Nashville: Abingdon Press, 1993), p. 76.

23. Ibid.

24. Ibid.

25. David Ng, "Rethinking Youth Ministry," in David S. Schuller, ed., *Rethinking Christian Education: Exploration in Theory and Practice* (St. Louis: Chalice Press, 1993), p. 85.

26. Ibid., p. 95.

27. Ibid., p. 96.

28. Roehlkepartain, *The Teaching Church*, p. 145.

29. Ibid.

30. Ibid.

31. Ibid., p. 186.

Bibliography

Astroth, Kirk A. "Are Youth at Risk?" *Journal of Extension. Volume* 31(3). Fall 1993. Printed version online: http://www.joe.org.

Atkinson, Harley. *Ministry with Youth in Crisis.* Birmingham, AL: Religious Education Press, 1997.

Balswick, Jack O., and Judith K. Balswick. *The Family: A Christian Perspective on the Contemporary Home.* Grand Rapids, MI: Baker Books, 1999.

Barna, George. *Real Teens: A Contemporary Snapshot of Youth Culture.* Ventura, CA: Regal Books, 2001.

Beaudoin, Tom. *Virtual Faith: The Irreverent Spiritual Quest of Generation X.* San Francisco: Jossey-Bass Publishers, Inc., 1998.

Billingsley, Andrew. *Climbing Jacob's Ladder: The Enduring Legacy of African American Families.* New York: Simon & Schuster, 1992.

———. *Mighty Like a River: The Black Church and Social Reform.* New York: Oxford University Press, 1999.

Borgman, Dean. *When Kumbaya Is Not Enough: A Practical Theology for Youth Ministry.* Peabody, MA: Hendrickson Press, 1999.

Boyd-Franklin, Nancy. *Black Families in Therapy: Understanding the African American Experience.* Second edition. New York: Guilford Press, 2003.

Boyd-Franklin, Nancy, and A. J. Franklin. *Boys into Men: Raising Our African American Teenage Sons.* New York: Dutton Books, 2001.

Boykin, Keith. *One More River to Cross: Black and Gay in America.* New York: Anchor Books, 1996.

Buttrick, George A. *The Interpreter's One-volume Commentary on the Bible: Introduction and Commentary for Each Book of the Bible Including the Apocrypha, with General Articles.* Nashville: Abingdon Press, 1990.

Card, Michael. *Basin and Towel*. Brentwood, TN: Sparrow Records, 1994.

Clements, Ronald E. "The Book of Deuteronomy: Introduction, Commentary, and Reflections." In *The New Interpreter's Bible*. Volume 2. Nashville: Abingdon Press, 1998.

Culpepper, R. Alan. "The Gospel of Luke: Introduction, Commentary, and Reflections." In *The New Interpreter's Bible*. Volume 9. Nashville: Abingdon Press, 1995.

Dodson, Jualynne. "Conceptualizations of Black Families." In Harriette Pipes McAdoo, ed., *Black Families*. Thousand Oaks, CA: Sage Publications, 1997.

Dunson, S. Miriam, ed. *Facing Forward in Older Adult Ministry*. Louisville, KY: Geneva Press, 1999.

Dyson, Drew A. *Faith-forming Junior High Ministry: Beyond Pizza 101*. Nashville: Abingdon Press, 2003.

Ellison, Christopher G. "Religious Involvement and the Subjective Quality of Family Life Among African Americans." In Robert Joseph Taylor, et al., eds., *Family Life in Black America*. Thousand Oaks, CA: Sage Publications, 1997.

Ellsworth, J'Anne. "Today's Adolescent: Addressing Existential Dread." Gale Group, 2001. Printed version online: http://www.findarticles.com.

Erikson, Erik. *Childhood and Society*. Second edition. New York: Norton & Company, 1964.

———. *Identity, Youth and Crises*. New York: W. W. Norton and Company, 1968.

Felder, Trunell D. "Counsel from Wise Others: Forming Wisdom Through Male Mentoring." In Anne E. Streaty Wimberly and Evelyn L. Parker, eds., *In Search of Wisdom: Faith Formation in the Black Church*. Nashville: Abingdon Press, 2002.

Fording, Richard D. "Laboratories of Democracy or Symbolic Politics." In Sanford F. Schram, Joe Soss, and Richard Fording, eds., *Race and the Politics of Welfare Reform*. Ann Arbor, MI: University of Michigan Press, 2003.

Freire, Paulo. *Education for Critical Consciousness*. New York: Continuum, 1973.

Hilliard, Asa, III. *The Maroon Within Us: Selected Essays on African American Community Socialization*. Baltimore, MD: Black Classic Press, 1995.

Hines, Paulette Moore. "The Family Life Cycle of African American Families." In Betty Carter and Monica McGoldrick, eds., *The Expanded Family Life Cycle: Individual, Family, and Social Perspectives.* Boston: Allyn and Bacon Publishers, 1999.

Ho, Man Keung. *Minority Children and Adolescents in Therapy.* Thousand Oaks, CA: Sage Publications, 1992.

Hofferth, S. L., and C. D. Hayes, eds. *Risking the Future.* Volume 2. Washington DC: National Academy Press, 1987.

hooks, bell. *Teaching to Transgress: Education as the Practice of Freedom.* New York: Vintage Books, 1994.

James, Richard K., and Burl Gilliland. *Crisis Intervention Strategies.* Pacific Grove, CA: Brooks/Cole Thompson Learning, 2001.

Jones, Lawrence N. "The Black Churches: A New Agenda." In Milton C. Sernett, ed., *Afro-American Religious History: A Documentary Witness.* Durham, NC: Duke University Press, 1985.

Jones, Reginald. *Black Psychology.* Berkeley, CA: Cobb & Henry Publishers, 1991.

Kesler, Jay. *Raising Responsible Kids: Ten Things You Can Do Now to Prepare for a Lifetime of Independence.* Brentwood, TN: Wolgemuth & Hyatt, Publishers, 1991.

Kitwana, Bakari. *The Hip Hop Generation: Young Blacks and the Crisis in African American Culture.* New York: BasicCivitas Books, 2002.

Kotesky, Ronald L. "Adolescence as a Cultural Invention." In Donald Ratcliff and James Davies, eds., *Handbook of Youth Ministry.* Birmingham, AL: Religious Education Press, 1991.

Kunjufu, Jawanza. *A Talk with Jawanza: Critical Issues in Educating African American Youth.* Chicago: African American Images, 1989.

———. *Restoring the Village, Values, and Commitment: Solutions for the Black Family.* Chicago: African American Images, 1996.

Lawrence, Rick. *Trendwatch: Insights That Fuel Authentic Youth Ministry.* Loveland, CO: Group Press, 2000.

Lincoln, C. Eric, and Lawrence H. Mamiya. *The Black Church in the African American Experience.* Durham, NC: Duke University Press, 1990.

Loder, Edward A. *Building an Intergenerational Church.* Louisville, KY: Westminster John Knox, 1999.

McWhirter, Jeffries J. et al. *At-Risk Youth: A Comprehensive Response—For Counselors, Teachers, Psychologists and Human Services Professionals.* Third edition. Belmont, CA: Brooks/Cole Publishers, 2003.

Merriam Webster's New Collegiate Dictionary. Tenth edition. Springfield, MA: Merriam-Webster, 1983.

Morris, Leon. *The Gospel According to John: The New International Commentary on the New Testament.* Grand Rapids, MI: William B. Eerdmans Publishing Company, 1971.

Mucherera, Tapiwa N. *Pastoral Care from a Third World Perspective: A Pastoral Theology of Care for the Urban Contemporary Shona in Zimbabwe.* New York: Peter Lang Publishers, 2001.

Myers, William H. "The Hermeneutical Dilemma of the African American Biblical Student." In Cain Hope Felder, ed., *Stony the Road We Trod: African American Biblical Interpretation.* Minneapolis: Fortress Press, 1991.

Neff, Blake J. "Communications and Relationships." In Donald Ratcliff and James A. Davies, eds., *Handbook of Youth Ministry.* Birmingham, AL: Religious Education Press, 1991.

Ng, David. "Rethinking Youth Ministry." In David S. Schuller, ed., *Rethinking Christian Education: Exploration in Theory and Practice.* St. Louis: Chalice Press, 1993.

Nichols, Sharon L., and Thomas L. Good. *America's Teenagers—Myths and Realities: Media Images, Schooling, and the Social Costs of Careless Indifference.* Mahwah, NJ: Lawrence Erlbaum Associates, Publishers, 2004.

Nichols, William C. *Treating People in Families: An Integrative Framework.* New York: Guilford Press, 1996.

Nobles, Wade. "Africanity: Its Role in Black Families." In Robert Staples, ed., *The Black Family: Essays and Studies.* Belmont, CA: Wadsworth, 1978.

Nouwen, Henri J. M. *With Open Hands.* Notre Dame, IN: Ave Maria Press, 1998.

Parker, Evelyn L. *Trouble Don't Last Always: Emancipatory Hope Among African American Adolescents.* Cleveland: Pilgrim Press, 2003.

Peters, Marie F. "Parenting in Black Families with Young Children: A Historical Perspective." In Harriette Pipes McAdoo, ed., *Black Families.* Thousand Oaks, CA: Sage Publications, 1997.

Peterson, Eugene H. *Like Dew Your Youth: Growing Up with Your Teenager.* Grand Rapids, MI: William B. Eerdmans Publishing Company, 2000.

Roehlkepartain, Eugene C. *The Teaching Church: Moving Christian Education to Center Stage.* Nashville: Abingdon Press, 1993.

Sandburg, Carl. "Names." Online: http://www.geocities.com.

Smith, Christian, et al. "Mapping American Adolescent Subjective Religiosity and Attitudes of Alienation Toward Religion: A Research Report," *Sociology of Religion,* Spring 2003. Reprinted version online through http://www.looksmart.com.

Smith, Yolanda Y. "Forming Wisdom Through Cultural Rootedness." In Anne E. Streaty Wimberly and Evelyn L. Parker, eds., *In Search of Wisdom: Faith Formation in the Black Church.* Nashville: Abingdon Press, 2002.

Somé, Malidome Patrice. *The Healing Wisdom of Africa: Finding Life Purpose Through Nature, Ritual and Community.* New York: Penguin Putnam, Inc., 1998.

Stevens, Joyce West. *Smart and Sassy: The Strengths of Inner-city Black Girls.* New York: Oxford University Press, 2002.

Stewart, Julia. *African Proverbs and Wisdom.* Secaucus, NJ: Carol Publishing Group, 1998.

Sudarkasa, Niara. "Interpreting the Africa Heritage in Afro-American Family Organization." In Harriette Pipes McAdoo, ed., *Black Families.* Thousand Oaks, CA: Sage Publications, 1997.

Tatum, Beverly Daniel. *"Why Are All the Black Kids Sitting Together in the Cafeteria?" And Other Conversations About Race.* New York: Basic Books, 1997.

Taylor, Robert Joseph, et al. "Recent Demographic Trends in African American Family Structure." In Robert Joseph Taylor, et al., eds., *Family Life in Black America.* Thousand Oaks, CA: Sage Publications, 1997.

The Barna Update, "Teens Change Their Tune Regarding Self and Church." April 23, 2002. Online: http://www.barna.org.

Thurman, Howard. *The Creative Encounter.* Richman, IN: Friends United Press, 1954.

United States Census Bureau. "The Black Population in the United States: March 2002." Washington, DC: The U.S. Department of Commerce, Economics and Statistics Administration, Census Bureau, April 2003.

Wade, Carole. *Psychology*. New York: HarperCollins College Publishers, 1996.

Warfield-Coppock, Nsenga. *Adolescent Rites of Passage*. Volume 1. Afrocentric Theory and Applications. Washington, DC: Baobab Associates, 1990.

Weems, Lovett H., Jr. *Church Leadership: Vision, Team, Culture, and Integrity*. Nashville: Abingdon Press, 1993.

West, Cornel. *Race Matters*. New York: Vintage Books, 1994.

Wimberly, Anne Streaty. "The Violence of Racism, The Strategy of Empowerment: Relational Hope and Co-action with Black Youth." *Black Theology: An International Journal* 1(1), November 2002: 53-66.

Wimberly, Anne E. Streaty, and Maisha I. Handy. "Conversations on Word and Deed: Forming Wisdom Through Female Mentoring." In Anne E. Streaty Wimberly and Evelyn L. Parker, eds., *In Search of Wisdom: Faith Formation in the Black Church*. Nashville: Abingdon Press, 2002.

Wimberly, Edward P. *Pastoral Counseling of African American Marriages and Families*. Louisville: Westminster John Knox Press, 1997.

————. *Relational Refugees: Alienation and Reincorporation in African American Churches and Communities*. Nashville: Abingdon Press, 2000.

Wimberly, Edward, and T. N. Mucherera. "Re-villaging, Crisis Theory, and the African Context." Presented at the Fourth Congress of the African Association of Pastoral Studies and Counseling in Yaounde Cameroon, July 27, 2001. Unpublished paper.

Wimberly, Edward, Anne Streaty Wimberly, and Annie Grace Chingonzo. "Pastoral Counselling, Spirituality and the Recovery of the Village Functions: African and African-American Correlates in the Practice of Pastoral Care and Counselling." In John Foskett and Emmanuel Lartey, eds., *Spirituality and Culture in Pastoral Care and Counselling: Voices from Different Contexts*. Cardiff, United Kingdom: Cardiff Academic Press, 2004.